UNDERSTANDING
HARMONY

UNDERSTANDING HARMONY

ROBERT L. JACOBS

'Musical form is not a series of mysteries
or trade secrets but is simply the
development of a power natural to the
human ear and the human mind'

R. VAUGHAN WILLIAMS

GREENWOOD PRESS, PUBLISHERS
WESTPORT, CONNECTICUT

Library of Congress Cataloging-in-Publication Data

Jacobs, Robert Louis.
  Understanding harmony.

  Reprint. Previously published: London ; New York :
Oxford University Press. 1969.
  Includes index.
  1. Harmony.   I. Title.
MT50.J17 1986   781.3   85-31691
ISBN 0-313-25092-8 (lib. bdg. : alk. paper)

First published 1958;
this book reprinted from 1969 edition

This reprint has been authorized by the Oxford University Press

Reprinted in 1986 by Greenwood Press
A division of Congressional Information Service, Inc.
88 Post Road West, Westport, Connecticut 06881

Printed in the United States of America

10 9 8 7 6 5 4 3 2 1

CONTENTS

AUTHOR'S NOTE

I acknowledge with gratitude the helpful advice and criticism which I received in the course of preparing this book from Dr Geoffrey Bush, Miss Madeleine Windsor, Eileen Aston, and, last not least, my publishers.

ACKNOWLEDGEMENTS

Acknowledgements are due to Hinrichsen Edition Ltd for permission to quote from Strauss's *Death and Transfiguration*; to Universal Edition for permission to quote from Bartók's Fifth Quartet, and from Schoenberg's Opus 15; to Durand et Cie, Paris, for permission to quote from Debussy's *La Cathédrale engloutie*; to Novello & Co. for permission to quote from Elgar's *Dream of Gerontius*; and to Boosey & Hawkes Ltd for permission to quote from Bartók's Violin Concerto, Stravinsky's *Rite of Spring*, and Britten's *Peter Grimes*.

INTRODUCTORY NOTE

THIS book is a re-issue of a hard-back published in 1958 under the title of *Harmony for the Listener*. The decision to change the title was taken in the light of its reception over the years. My object was to provide inquiring listeners, able to read musical quotations, with a general understanding of the role of harmony in music. Because I was treating the subject in a fresh way—not providing yet another re-hash for popular consumption of textbook harmony, but taking harmony, as it were, out of the textbook and opening a window on the whole by showing its interconnection with melody, form, style, and the history and psychology of music—I hoped that I might also be providing something of value to musical students, bound to the 'set subject' of the examination syllabus. This hope has proved to be justified, and so I have taken the opportunity of the book's re-issue as a paper-back to replace the original title, *Harmony for the Listener*, by the more comprehensive one, *Understanding Harmony*.

I have also taken the opportunity to rectify a few minor errors, re-word a few passages, and add an Appendix, 'Recommended Reading'. The only other change calling for specific mention is again one of title: the penultimate chapter, 'Some Trends of Twentieth-century Harmony', I have re-named 'Some Trends of Early Twentieth-century Harmony'. In that chapter I survey twentieth-century trends in the light of their relation to classical harmony, the book's principal concern. In 1958, when it was published, I could claim that the survey covered the features 'generally recognized as the most important and characteristic' of the century. Today's characteristic trend is the wholesale innovation of Boulez, Stockhausen, and John Cage, involving a re-thinking of the very nature of musical art. Bearing as they do no relation to classical harmony, the works of these composers, and of the many influenced by them, lie outside the scope of that chapter, and so I have changed its title.   '

A final word is called for by the summaries appended to every chapter save the final one. Having been at pains to present my material in an orderly, intelligible way, beginning with elementary topics and advancing stage by stage to complex ones, I appended them in order to enable the reader to look back at the end of each chapter and obtain a rapid bird's-eye view of its contents before proceeding further. Whether he cares to avail himself of the opportunity is a matter for him to decide.

CHAPTER I

The Logic in Melody

'MELODY', so runs the tag, 'is the soul of music.' And of course it is. The music that

> . . . when soft voices die,
> Vibrates in the memory . . .

is the melody, not the harmony. It is the tune that haunts. That melody and harmony are interwoven we shall see in the next chapter (and indeed throughout the whole of this book). Yet melody is what we remember, melody is the 'soul', because it is through it that music's meaning is apprehended, through it that it makes sense.

From which it follows that it might be wise to approach a study of harmony through that of melody. And that one might do worse than take as one's starting point the elementary, yet fundamental, question which the tag 'melody is the soul of music' raises. What, one might start by asking, constitutes that 'meaning' apprehended through melody? A meaning implies a logic; a logic implies a train of thought; a train of thought implies a progression towards an anticipated, predetermined goal. How can this apply to melody?—to melody consisting not of meaningful words, but of mere notes of this or that pitch, arranged to follow each other according to this or that rhythmic pattern?

Let us start by considering not a melody as a whole, but the phrases of which melodies consist. Regarding them, let us point to a fact so obvious that it is often passed over as not worth remarking upon, namely, that the meaning of a phrase, whatever this meaning is, is a thing which builds up during the course of the phrase and does not finally reveal itself until the last note has been heard. That this is so we can see by making the simple experiment of lopping off the last note of a familiar phrase: **Ex. I**

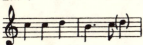

The effect is rather as though one had suddenly been summoned out of a theatre at the climax of an exciting play five minutes before the fall of the curtain. If this were to happen we would not console ourselves with the thought that those five minutes, being after all only five minutes, were expendable; we would feel that, having missed the climax of the play, our *whole* evening had been spoilt. Similarly the *whole* of that phrase is spoilt. As the play builds up, bit by bit, gathering tension and finally releasing it in the last five minutes, so the phrase builds up note by note until it comes to rest upon the final one. In fact, one could legitimately say that we experience the phrase as *a movement to a goal, the goal being the final note.*

This established, we are now able to put our question into a more precise and, as we shall see, more rewarding form. What, we can ask, is the nature of the logic which links these goals to which the various phrases of a melody move?—which links these goals, so that the melody as a whole assumes a total meaning?

Let us attempt to find an answer by returning to the tune 'God save the Queen' and studying it phrase by phrase. If we do this we shall discover that though no two of the phrases are the same, though the notes and rhythms of which they consist vary in manifold ways, nevertheless the individual effect which each phrase makes, notwithstanding its individuality, can be broadly and obviously classed as either one or other of the two following kinds: either the phrase sounds more or less complete in itself, or else it sounds more or less incomplete. Thus the first

Ex. 2

phrase  sounds incomplete;

the second phrase has an air of completeness:

Ex. 3

similarly, and even more so, the third phrase:

The next three phrases all sound more or less incomplete:

The last phrase is the most positively complete of all:

It is not difficult to see what the factor is which has made it possible to draw this broad obvious distinction between these phrases all differing from each other: it is whether the last note, the goal, of each phrase is the same or not as one particular note, namely the C on which the melody ends. It is when they are the same that the phrase sounds complete, when they are different, incomplete. In relation to this particular note the others seem to focus themselves. To put it another way: the C seems to be drawing an invisible straight line through the melody in relation to which its notes are 'placed'; thus:

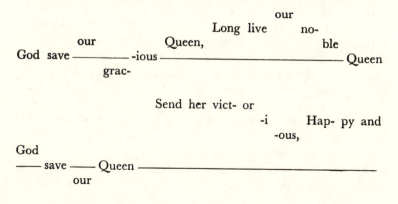

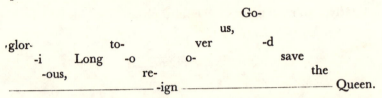

We can now begin to answer our question: What is the logic in melody? We can assume that it is a logic which has something to do with the fact (1) that each phrase of a melody moves to its final note as to a goal, (2) that a melody has a central *tonic* note (as such a central note is called), in relation to which all the others are 'placed', and (3) that, apart from the multitude of other factors distinguishing them, phrases differ broadly in sounding complete or incomplete according to whether their final note is the same as the tonic of the melody. We can catch a first glimpse of our answer if we now point out that the incomplete phrase sets in train a logic which demands that its departure from the 'invisible line' of the tonic shall be reversed, that sooner or later it be followed by a phrase returning to the 'invisible line'. When this happens, logic is satisfied and we feel a sense of completeness and fulfilment. The logic, in fact, might be described as a departure-in-order-to-enjoy-the-pleasure-of-the-return.

Presented in this way it seems a disappointingly petty logic, a mere mouse emerging from a mountain of tiresome exposition. But this is only our first glimpse. Drawing nearer, we soon see what a fascinatingly involved logic it really is. In the first place the crudely simple relation between two notes of 'being the same' or 'not being the same'—the only one which we have yet considered—is, of course, very far indeed from the only one: for all save the tone-deaf there also exists a whole gamut of *degrees of likeness and unlikeness* between two notes. Thus the incomplete phrase will sound not merely incomplete but *more or less* incomplete according to how like or unlike its final note is to the tonic. Or to put it another way: the incomplete phrase's departure from the 'invisible line' of the tonic will be more than merely a departure, it will be a departure *to a definite point more or less far away.*

Another factor is that differences exist in the way one note *follows* another. A note may be felt to pull to the note coming after—as it were, to want to be followed by it—or it may go to it reluctantly. This brings a further differentiation to the incomplete phrase: it means that the departure of the phrase to the point which may be near or far from the 'invisible line' *will sound more or less decisive*, according to whether the final note, the goal of the phrase, is pulled to by the note coming before it.

In the next section we shall examine these various relationships between two notes. Meanwhile, let us conclude this one by baptizing with its technical name this logic of melody we have been catching a first sight of. Since its source is the melody's tonic the logic is called *tonality*. And the pair of notes at the end of a phrase, i.e. the goal and the note before, is called the *cadence* of a phrase. These are vitally important terms in the technical vocabulary of music—indeed so important that I can say without exaggeration that my chief purpose in writing this book is to reveal their implications.

SUMMARY OF CHAPTER I

Since it is only in the context of a melody that harmonies acquire musical meaning, some preliminary study of melody is called for. The elementary question must be considered: what is the nature of the logic which imparts meaning to a melody?

Consider the phrases of which melodies consist:

(1) The final note of a phrase is experienced as the goal to which the others have been moving.

(2) A phrase sounds more or less complete or incomplete in itself. The criterion is whether or not its final note is the same as the central 'tonic' note of the melody, drawing through it an 'invisible line'.

Since the ear demands that an incomplete phrase should sooner or later be followed by a complete one, reversing the previous movement away from the tonic's 'invisible line', and takes pleasure in this when it happens, the logic of melody might be described as a departure-in-order-to-enjoy-the-pleasure-of-the-return.

Two factors make this logic, on the face of it so simple, fascinatingly involved:

(1) Between two notes of different pitch there exists a whole gamut of degrees of likeness and unlikeness. The incomplete phrase therefore sounds *more or less* incomplete according to how like or unlike its final note is to the tonic.

(2) Differences exist in the ways which notes succeed each other: a note may pull to its successor or go to it reluctantly. This brings a further differentiation to the effect of a phrase, since it means that its movement to its final note sounds more or less decisive according to whether it is pulled to or not by the penultimate one.

The logic is called *tonality*, and the pair of notes at the end of the phrase the *cadence*.

CHAPTER II

The Qualities of Intervals

WHAT makes possible a range of relationships between pairs of notes over and above the crude one of 'being the same' or 'not being the same' is the fact that each of the many differences of pitch that can exist—in other words, each interval—conveys a specific individual quality. A two-note progression may or may not convey the effect of a pull to the second note and the pull may be more or less strong. A two-note chord may be more or less agreeable or disagreeable. In this chapter it is my purpose, as it were, to enter the laboratory—to remove intervals from the context of live music, inspect them as things-in-themselves, describe their qualities and accordingly classify them.

Although I assume the reader of this book to be conversant with the intervals, for the purposes of this chapter I shall refer to them not only by their usual names, but also in terms of the notes of the major scale of C. Thus I shall call a fifth the C–G' interval, the stroke after G indicating that it is the upper of the two notes. (Were the stroke after C—thus, C'–G—then C would be the upper note and the interval accordingly a fourth.)

On page 8 is a table of the intervals within the octave, listed according to their size, with a sample of each from the major scale of C and, for the benefit of the reader whose memory may need refreshing, an indication of their size in terms of semitones.

Each of these intervals, *experienced as a thing in itself*, has, I said, a specific quality—as specific as the colour of a delphinium or the taste of a strawberry. *Experienced in the context of music* it is of course another matter. If you are attuned to Schoenberg, if you are captivated by the force of his thematic design and contrapuntal skill, you will spontaneously accept the dissonant intervals he employs as the necessary, inevitable concomitant of his art. Inspect those same intervals in the laboratory, divorced from the overpowering associations of Schoenberg's music, and you will agree that in themselves they are very unpleasant. The findings of musical psychologists leave no

2

TABLE OF INTERVALS

Name of interval			Sample from scale of C major	Size in terms of semitones
Minor second	..	..	B–C'	1
Major second	..	..	C–D'	2
Minor third ..	..	..	E–G'	3
Major third ..	..	..	C–E'	4
Perfect fourth	..	..	C–F'	5
Tritone[1]	..	..	F–B'	6
Perfect fifth ..	..	..	C–G'	7
Minor sixth ..	..	..	E–C'	8
Major sixth ..	..	..	G–E'	9
Minor seventh	..	..	D–C'	10
Major seventh	..	..	C–B'	11
Octave	..	..	C–C'	12

[1] The tritone is thus called because it spans three tones. The interval is also known as the augmented fourth and as the diminished fifth, according to the context in which it occurs.

doubt that, differ though we may outside the laboratory, inside it the qualities of intervals are perceived more or less uniformly. In my experience of giving interval tests such disagreements as do arise boil down to quarrels about words. Thus frequent bones of contention are the intervals of a fourth and fifth, whose curiously bare neutral character is very hard to describe.

In what follows I am going to assume that my perception of the qualities of intervals is typical of most people's. Should the reader find himself disagreeing, I request him to leave it an open question whether the difference is due to a temperamental quirk of his or of mine, or whether it is due to a desire to have the same thing said in another way.

Although interval-qualities are *sui generis*, purely musical phenomena, unique and ultimately unaccountable, they are nevertheless intimately connected with two general factors, one psycho-physiological, the other acoustic, each of which throws some light upon their nature and in relation to which it is therefore convenient to consider them.

The psycho-physiological factor is the expressive functioning of the human voice. Two obvious characteristics of this functioning, affecting intervals generally, must be borne in mind. The first is that excitement causes us to raise the voice and relaxation to lower it; thus rising interval-progressions create tension and falling ones reduce it. The second is that—it being a biological tendency to employ the minimum energy to achieve an end—we keep our intonations within a small range for the purposes of everyday utterance and increase it only under the pressure of exceptional emotion; thus close interval-progressions tend to sound normal and wide ones to have an arresting, spectacular quality.

The acoustic factor is the complex phenomenon of the overtones. It is a factor different in kind from the psycho-physiological: there the connexion was with habits of utterance bearing only indirectly upon music; here it is with a phenomenon arising purely out of the nature of musical sound and affecting us purely in virtue of our musical faculty.

Concerning this complex acoustic phenomenon we only need to bear in mind three facts. The first two are elementary, namely that

(1) a note of definite pitch is produced by a sound-wave oscillating regularly;

(2) the more rapid the oscillation, the higher the pitch. Thus if you talk in front of an oscillograph the instrument records a jagged series of waves:

If you pitch your voice to hold a musical note the jagged series becomes an even one:

If you take a higher note, the curves become more frequent:

(3) The third fact is harder to envisage (indeed so hard that all a layman can do is accept it unintelligently as a phenomenon defying imagination). When a vibrating substance—

say, the length of wire stretched to give the pianist his middle C
—is set into motion its vibrations do not, as one would expect,
merely take the form of a series of total movements of the
whole wire (thus ⸺⸺⸺⸺); there also occurs a series
of subsidiary vibrations at higher speeds along different fractions
of the wire's length. Half the wire is vibrating at twice the
speed of the total vibration, a third at three times the speed,
a fourth four times, and so on through ever diminishing
fractions. Roughly this process of *compound* or *fractional* vibrations, as it is called, could be pictured thus:

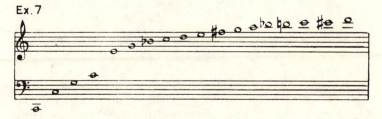

Total Vibration

Vibrating as they do at different speeds, these subsidiary
oscillations necessarily produce a series of subsidiary tones of
different pitch. These so-called *harmonics* or *overtones* or *partials*
are not normally distinguishable—they blend with the fundamental note produced by the total vibration. But—as the
famous nineteenth-century German physicist, Helmholtz, discovered—the tone-quality of a sounded note varies according
to their number and relative strength. Helmholtz drew the
general conclusion that '. . . notes which are accompanied by
a moderately loud series of the lower partial tones up to about
the sixth are more harmonious and musical'.[1]

Taking the C two octaves below middle C as the fundamental, the series of its overtones—the Harmonic Series—is as
follows (for convenience's sake I set it out as a succession of
separate notes):

Ex. 7

[1] Alexander Wood, *The Physics of Music* (1944), p. 70.

If we sound this fundamental loudly on a grand piano and hold down the pedal we can faintly distinguish its first five overtones, i.e. the C an octave above, the G a fifth higher, middle C, the E a major third higher, the G a minor third higher. If we play these notes together as a chord:

Ex.8

the effect will be ideally rich and satisfying. Which, of course, is what one would expect: if the rich tone-quality of an instrument is due to the prominence of its lower overtones, one would expect the chord in which these overtones were realized as notes to have an ideally satisfying, 'co-sounding' (if one may coin the term), consonant quality. It is as though, in making manifest to the ear as harmony what before it could only hear as tone-quality one were taking a cue from Nature. The chord in question is indeed sometimes referred to as 'Nature's Chord'.

If we spread this chord out into an arpeggio we find that the chordal quality of consonance translates itself in the progression of the notes:

Ex.9

And if we examine the quality of the interval formed by any pair of the notes of the arpeggio, we find that though each pair, either as chord or as progression, has its distinctive quality—is more or less pleasing or unpleasing, smooth or harsh—yet they all have in common a quality of consonance. The quality is present, however uncomfortably wide the jump of the progression and irrespective of whether it is a rising or a falling one.

Not that the psycho-physiological factor is not operative here; not that the effect is the same however wide the interval or whether it rises or falls. The case is not so simple: *both* factors operate. Since, however, the intervals in question share the acoustic quality of consonance I shall regard them as forming a separate 'acoustic' category of their own. I shall consider them first, describing as best I can their respective individual qualities, and then deal similarly with the remaining intervals.

The intervals of this 'acoustic' category I shall consider in four groups as follows:

(1) the octave  ;

(2) the C–G' interval of a fifth:  and its reverse

position the C'–G interval of a fourth  ;

(3) the C–E' interval of a major third:  and

its reverse position the C'–E interval of a minor

sixth:  ;

(4) the E–G' interval of a minor third:  and

its reverse position the E'–G interval of a major

sixth:  .

The justification of this grouping is, as we shall see, that the chords and progressions of each group have significant effects in common.

The first group, the octave, can be briefly dismissed. So strong is the affinity between fundamental and first overtone

that in the chord the note of the overtone adds no element of
'otherness' to the fundamental: the chord is not experienced
as a chord, i.e. as a combination of two different notes, but
rather as the amplification of a single note. Similarly in the
progression: one note is felt to be merely the duplication of the
other at a different register, to be the same, only 'higher' or
'lower' as the case may be. Hence the ease and naturalness of
the interval despite its unvocal width—and hence its characterlessness. Nothing new seems to be happening. It is as though a
note were merely looking at its own reflection in a mirror.

The second group, the fifth and fourth, cannot be so simply
described. In the chord of the fifth the overtone-note—here the
second overtone—does add an element of 'otherness' to the
fundamental: the effect is definitely that of a combination of
two different notes. Yet the chord, for all its consonance, is not
satisfying. It is as though the two notes were not different
enough, as though the affinity between fundamental and overtone were too strong; whatever the cause, its effect has something of that characterlessness which we noted in the octave.
It is bare and flavourless.

As a progression, on the other hand, the interval of a fifth
presents a most striking contrast to that of the octave. Here
there is no question of feeling one note merely as the duplication
of another at a different register. Each moves to the other as to
a new position, the acoustic affinity making itself felt in that
the movement conveys a powerful effect of dynamic attraction
between the two. In other words, *they seem to pull to each other.*
As one would expect, the progression from overtone to fundamental—from G to C—pulls more decisively than that from
fundamental to overtone—from C to G. The fundamental,
since it *is* the fundamental, exerts the stronger attraction. We
shall see later that these pulls play an important part in the
classical key system.

All of this applies equally to the progression of a fourth,
formed as it is by the same pair of notes. What distinguishes it
from the fifth is the psycho-physiological factor, namely, that
being slightly the closer of the two, it is slightly the more
comfortable and natural progression. As a chord, however, the
fourth differs more than slightly from the fifth, since it inverts
the natural position of fundamental and overtone, putting the

fundamental not, as in the fifth, below, but above the overtone. It shares with the fifth that effect of 'not being different enough', of bareness and flavourlessness. But it is at the same time less consonant.

Our third group, the major third and minor sixth, conveys an effect of consonance utterly different in kind from that of the octave and of the fifth and fourth. Consider first the chord of the major third, C–E'. There is no question here of the notes 'not being different enough' and the chord consequently being bare and flavourless. Here the affinity between fundamental and overtone—now the fourth overtone—expresses itself in another way altogether, namely in that the two combine to produce a chord *sensuously pleasing and satisfying in itself*. It is indeed the presence of this note which imparts to 'Nature's Chord' quoted above (Ex. 8) its *ideally* consonant quality; the presence of this note which causes the combination of C with G and E to become a chord transcending the separate sounds which compose it, to become in Browning's famous words:

'. . . not a fourth sound, but a star'.

In the progression of the major third we feel this sensuously pleasing satisfying quality of the chord, as it were, 'spread out'. It does not pull, as fifths and fourths do; instead it gladdens and charms.

These attributes of the major third are still present, though modified, in the minor sixth, C'–E, both as chord and as progression. They are modified because the chord inverts the natural position of the notes and because the progression of the interval is wide. Even so they still assert themselves.

In our fourth group, the minor third and major sixth, we have the fourth overtone, E, combining with the second overtone, G, instead of with the fundamental. Though not so spectacular as the major third, this combination also produces a sensuously pleasing chord and a gladdening progression. The quality is perhaps more pronounced in the chord of the major sixth, since here the second overtone, G, is below the fourth one, E, and thus the natural position of the notes preserved; on the other hand the progression of the close interval of a minor third is smoother. (To avoid misunderstanding, I owe it to the reader to point out that the quality of sadness generally attributed to the chord of the minor third does not inhere in the interval *as such*—which is what concerns us in this chapter—but arises from its presence in a specific harmonic context, the minor triad, to be discussed in due course.)

*   *   *   *

The remaining intervals divide easily into two clearly defined groups. Into one fall the major seventh (C–B'), the tritone (F–B'), and the minor seventh (C'–D), each of which is more or less dissonant as chord and more or less disagreeable as progression. The major seventh is excruciating in both respects; the tritone (which medieval theorists dubbed the 'diabolus in musica') perhaps somewhat less so—it is a matter of opinion. The minor seventh, on the other hand, is comparatively harmonious and smooth.

Into the other group fall the two closest intervals of a tone and semitone, both of which are dissonant as chords, the semitone excruciatingly so, but on the other hand as progressions eminently smooth and vocal.

The importance of the psycho-physiological factor in these two closest progressions is evident in a characteristic which they share and which distinguishes them from all the other intervals we have been discussing, namely *the sharply different effect of their rising and their falling forms*. Not that the rise and fall of other progressions do not convey different effects, the rise creating a feeling of tension, the fall of relaxation; but here the difference is so great that it alters the whole quality of the interval. Consider first the falling progression of a tone. D falls naturally to C as though it were attracted to it—in fact with something of that pull which we observed in the progressions of the fifth and fourth. In the rising progression this effect of a pull between the two notes completely disappears: C rises reluctantly to D. It seems loth to exert itself.

In the progression of the semitone the psycho-physiological factor is even more marked. The fall of this, the closest interval of the scale, is so like the motion of the voice gliding downwards in a sigh or wail or moan that its effect is inherently pathetic. Think how eloquently Moussorgsky used this interval—simply this interval—in the lament of the Idiot in *Boris Godunov*:

Ex. 10

Oh!_   Oh!_   Oh!_   Oh!_

In the rising form of the progression the pull goes powerfully upward. When the lower note is accented the effect is still pathetic; it is as though the accented note were yearning to raise itself to the level of the note to follow—as witness this figure from *Tristan*, the opera *par excellence* of yearning:

Ex. 11

But when the lower note is not accented, as in the third phrase of the National Anthem:

Ex. 12

the pathos is gone and instead there is an easy, inevitable, sharply decisive thrust to the upper note—in fact the most compelling pull of all. With what other psycho-physiological or acoustic factor this pull can be connected it would be beside the point to speculate here. Let us be content to accept it as a *fait accompli*; and let us mark it well, for it is one of the most significant progressions of classical harmony.[1]

In conclusion I append a list of the intervals and summary of their qualities as set forth above.

---

[1] Having dwelt at such length in this chapter on the acoustic basis of consonance, I owe it to the reader to remark that, because this basis exists, it does not follow that a system of harmony can be scientifically derived from the laws of acoustics. No such system can be, if only for the reason that, as we shall see below, in the context of music the properties of chords become compounded with melody and rhythm in which other forces operate.

THE QUALITIES OF INTERVALS

	As chord	As progression	
Acoustic' intervals		*rising*	*falling*
Octave ..	characterless	characterless	characterless
Fifth	bare	pulls powerfully	pulls powerfully
Fourth ..	bare, but less consonant than the fifth	pulls powerfully	pulls powerfully
Major third ⎱ .. Minor sixth ⎰	sensuously pleasing	sensuously pleasing	sensuously pleasing
Minor third ⎱ .. Major sixth ⎰	sensuously pleasing	sensuously pleasing	sensuously pleasing
Other intervals			
Major seventh ⎱ Tritone ⎰	acutely dissonant	acutely disagreeable	acutely disagreeable
Minor seventh	mildly dissonant	mildly disagreeable	mildly disagreeable
Tone	mildly dissonant	rises reluctantly	pulls fairly powerfully
Semitone ..	acutely dissonant	pulls very powerfully	pulls with an effect of pathos

SUMMARY OF CHAPTER II

The purpose of the chapter is to take intervals 'into the laboratory' and examine their qualities as chords and as progressions.

Two general factors serve as a basis for classification:

(1) A vocal psycho-physiological factor.

Since when excited we raise the voice and when relaxed lower it, rising interval-progressions generally create tension and falling ones reduce it.

Since the intonations of the voice are normally kept within a small range, close interval-progressions generally sound normal and wide ones arresting and spectacular.

(2) An 'acoustic' factor, i.e. the phenomenon of compound vibration giving rise to 'co-sounding' consonant overtones.

The acoustic consonant intervals fall into four groups:

(1) The Octave (C–C')

As chord

The acoustic affinity is so strong that the chord is experienced merely as the amplification of the fundamental. Its quality is bare and characterless.

As progression

Despite its abnormal width the progression is easy and characterless.

(2) The Fifth (C–G') and Fourth (C'–G)

The fifth as chord

The effect is that of a combination of two different notes, nevertheless, like that of the octave, the effect is bare, owing to the close acoustic affinity of fundamental and overtone.

The fifth as progression

Unlike the octave, the acoustic affinity manifests itself in an effect of dynamic attraction between the two notes. The overtone pulls more powerfully to the fundamental than the fundamental to the overtone.

The fourth as chord

Similar to the fifth, but less consonant since it inverts the acoustic relation of the two notes, the fundamental being placed above the overtone.

The fourth as progression

Similar to the fifth, but, being a closer interval, more vocal.

(3) The Major Third (C–E') and Minor Sixth (C'–E)

The major third as chord

Here the effect of the acoustic affinity is a chord which is sensuously pleasing.

The major third as progression

The pleasing effect of the chord persists in the progression. It does not pull as do the fifths and fourths.

The minor sixth as chord

Similar to the major third but slightly less pleasing, since it inverts the acoustic relation of the notes.

The minor sixth as progression

The pleasing effect of the chord persists, despite the unvocal width of the progression.

(4) The Minor Third (E–G') and Major Sixth (E'–G)

The minor third as chord

Again a sensuously pleasing effect.

The minor third as progression

Again the pleasing effect of the chord persists in the progression.

The major sixth as chord

A more positively pleasing effect than that of the minor third, since the latter inverts the acoustic relation of the notes.

The major sixth as progression

The pleasing effect of the chord persists, despite the unvocal width of the progression.

The remaining intervals fall into two groups:

(1) The tritone (F–B'), the major seventh (C–B'), and the minor seventh (D–C') which are in varying degrees both dissonant as chords and disagreeable as progressions.

(2) The closest intervals of a tone and a semitone, which are in varying degrees dissonant as chords, but on the other hand smooth and vocal as progressions.

The significance of the psycho-physiological factor is apparent in the contrast between the rising and the falling form of the tone and semitone progressions:

The tone falls with a pull, but rises reluctantly.

The semitone falls with a pull, which, since the progression closely resembles the intonations of the voice, is inherently pathetic.

The semitone also rises with a pull. If the lower note is accented the pull has a pathetic quality; but if the upper one is accented the pull conveys a thrust of unique power and decisiveness.

CHAPTER III

The Logic in Melody (*continued*)

THE purpose of this chapter is to show how the qualities of intervals, just discussed, are harnessed to the logic of tonality in the context of an actual piece of music.

Let us start by recalling the findings of our first chapter in regard to this logic. It resided, we saw, in four factors:

(1) a melody has a central 'tonic' note drawing, as I put it, an 'invisible line' in relation to which the other notes 'place' themselves;

(2) the final note of a phrase is felt as the goal of the others;

(3) a phrase sounds more or less complete or incomplete according to the relationship—or, as we may now say, the interval—between its final note and the tonic;

(4) the degree of completeness or incompleteness of a phrase is also determined by the interval between its penultimate and final cadence-notes.

* * * *

Now that we are about to leave the artificial laboratory we must briefly take note of certain obvious general factors, not observable there, governing our perception of intervals in the real context of living music.

One such is the rhythmic beat, the recurring '*one*-two' or '*one*-two-three' which in one form or another governs all the music we listen to. The accent on the 'one', the so-called 'strong' beat, forces us to concentrate our attention on the successive 'strong' beats of a phrase—on, say, the C and B of the first two bars of the National Anthem:

Ex. 13

Indeed to all intents and purposes these two notes are experienced as forming an interval, *and this notwithstanding the existence*

of notes between them forming intervening intervals. This capacity for jumping over intervening notes and singling out particular pairs as especially significant, this 'selective awareness', as one might term it, of certain intervals, has a direct bearing on the logic of tonality. It is indeed the condition on which the logic depends for its very being. Thus we are 'selectively aware' of the interval between the phrase's final note and the melody's tonic. Again, since the phrase's final note is experienced as the goal of the others we must also somehow be 'selectively aware' of the respective intervals which it forms with each of them. And yet (at this point the sheer complexity of the process begins to overwhelm us!) through all this we continue to trace the course of the phrase from note to note and feel what we call its 'curve' in the rise and fall of the various intervals as they succeed each other. The curve stamps itself upon our mind so that we remember it and relate it to the curve of the next phrase and the next until at the end the total curve of the melody as a whole has been grasped.

After this brief glimpse into the wonderfully complicated workings of the musical mind (yours, reader, and mine), we are now in a position to carry out the purpose of this chapter, that of showing how individual intervals are harnessed to the logic of tonality. We can do this best by turning once again to the tune of 'God save the Queen' and analysing some of its features in the light of what we have learnt of the qualities of intervals. We now have a better tool of analysis than the crude criterion, which was all we could use in the first chapter, of whether notes were 'the same' or 'not the same'.

Let us begin by taking the first 'incomplete' phrase of the tune, just quoted, and examining the part which the intervals concerned play in determining the quality of its 'incompleteness'. Thus the final note of the phrase is D, which forms with C, the tonic, the interval of a tone. We saw that as a chord this interval is dissonant, and it is its chordal character here which is operative. D has no close overtone-relationship with C: going from C to D the phrase accordingly seems to be landing us in a strange region—seems, in fact, very 'incomplete' indeed. Just how 'incomplete' we realize when we compare the effect of the phrase to that of a similar one ending on one of C's consonant overtone-notes, i.e. on E or on G:

Ex. 14

The effect of 'incompleteness' here is not only less pronounced, but quite different *in kind*. There is no sense of landing in a strange region, but rather of remaining at home and, as it were, merely moving into another room. Or one might express the difference by reverting to our former image and saying that with D as the goal of the phrase the effect is that of a movement pointing decisively away from the tonic's 'invisible

Ex. 15

line'  while with E or G as

the goal it is rather that of a movement to a line parallel with that of the tonic:

Ex. 16

Indeed, it is as though, suspended above the tonic's 'invisible line', there were two fainter ones running parallel with it at the level of these two overtones.

Now consider the interval of the phrase's two cadence-notes, that of a rising tone. We saw that the rising tone, unlike the falling one, conveys no thrust, that it rises 'reluctantly'. In the context this 'reluctant' quality reinforces the effect of 'incompleteness'. The fact that not only are we landing in a strange region, but landing there reluctantly, reinforces the sense of its strangeness.

So much for the first phrase of the tune. Let us now consider the others, somewhat more briefly.

Ex. 17

The second phrase: 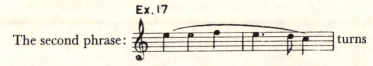 turns

away from the strange region reached by the first one and swings the melody back to rest upon the tonic's 'invisible line'.

It *swings* it back: where previously the interval of the cadence-notes was the reluctant rising tone, now it is the decisive falling

Ex. 18

one. The third phrase, , as though to

wipe out every memory of that initial journey abroad, swings back to the tonic yet again, and even more decisively, approaching it as it does through the rising semitone, the most powerfully thrusting of all the intervals.

This rising semitone here is, as a matter of fact, the pivot upon which the whole tune hinges. The tonic having been effectively re-affirmed after that initial departure to D, the next three phrases venture further afield (from G to E, F to D, and E back again to G):

Ex. 19

The last phrase, after touching A, the highest point yet reached, falls steeply to a final landing on the tonic.

Ex. 20

What that rising semitone does—and no other interval could do it—is to re-plant the tonic firmly in our minds in view of the further excursions to come. It is no exaggeration to say that without this interval at this pivotal point the *total* effect of the tune is destroyed. The reader can test the truth of this for himself by imagining some other interval substituted, for example A–C':

Ex. 21

3

It is time to draw to a close this analysis of the National Anthem and with it this chapter, for now we have the preliminary knowledge of tonality and of the qualities of intervals and of the connexion between the two, which we need for the purpose of this book. Having occupied this vantage ground, we are in a position to advance forthwith into the territory of harmony proper.

SUMMARY OF CHAPTER III

The purpose of the chapter is to show how the qualities of intervals are harnessed to the logic of tonality.

Before this can be shown it is necessary to take note of the manner in which intervals are perceived in the context of live music. Hearing a melody is more than a matter of perceiving a number of successive intervals: pairs of notes can be grasped as forming intervals, even though intervening notes may divide them. Thus the notes which occur on the successive 'strong' beats of the bar are perceived as intervals. In the same way the ear is 'selectively aware' of the interval between the phrase's final note and the tonic, and of the intervals between the notes of the phrase and the phrase's final note.

Analysis of the constituent phrases of the National Anthem shows how the degree of 'completeness' or 'incompleteness' of each is determined by the nature of the interval at the cadence and of that between the final note and tonic. It shows further that the structure of the tune, moving away from the tonic, returning to it at the second and third phrase, and subsequently moving still further away, hinges upon the decisive semitonal thrust of the cadence of the third phrase.

CHAPTER IV

The 'Vertical' and the 'Horizontal' Aspects of Harmony

I SAID in my introduction that this book is not intended to be a comprehensive textbook of harmony dealing with all the various contingencies that arise in the handling of chords, but only as a guide to fundamental principles. These fundamental principles have their source in the logic of tonality just described.

The first stage of our advance into the field of harmony proper must be a brief general consideration of how the blobs of simultaneously sounded notes which we call chords are perceived when we hear them strung together in the context of a melody. When this happens we do not perceive them as a series of harmonic blobs, each a separate thing-in-itself; the harmonies merge into and enrich the significance of the notes of the melody. To put it diagrammatically, what we perceive is not

but rather

But this is not all. As the melody unfolds what we hear is not merely a harmonized 'God', harmonized 'save', harmonized 'our' and so on. Beneath the tune we also hear subordinate lines of melody created by the intervals formed by the constituent notes of the supporting chords. This diagram therefore depicts the experience more accurately:

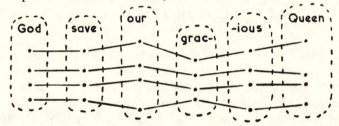

Once again in fact we meet that phenomenon of 'selective awareness' encountered in the previous chapter; once again we find the mind working simultaneously on different planes. On the *vertical* plane, indicated by the dotted lines of our diagram, we perceive chords as pillars of notes supporting the notes of the melody; on the *horizontal* plane we perceive them as forming lower strands of melody. Which of the two planes we perceive more vividly varies from work to work (and indeed from portion to portion of a single work). In an unaccompanied motet for two voices our perception is horizontal rather than vertical; what engages us is the interaction of the two melodic lines, not the two-note chords they keep forming. On the other hand in a piece such as 'God save the Queen', conceived of as a harmonized single melody, the reverse is true: it is the harmonization which engages us, not the layers of subordinate melody.

In the next chapter, in which we shall begin our discussion of the chords of the major scale, our point of view will be exclusively vertical. The chords we shall discuss will be concords. A discord, i.e. a chord dissatisfying in itself and hence requiring some other chord to follow it, has (with the exception of one important class of discord to be considered in due course) no independent vertical significance: its structure and character are entirely the creation of the melodic line in which it functions. Concords, on the other hand, have an independent significance. As chords they have in their own right a specific satisfying character and this character has an important bearing upon the logic of tonality. Our first task, therefore, must be to re-visit the laboratory and, as we laid out on the table the intervals, lay out the concords, analyse their structure and as best we can describe their character.

SUMMARY OF CHAPTER IV

Chords are perceived upon two planes:

(1) a vertical plane, in which they are experienced as pillars of notes merging with the notes of a melody;

(2) a horizontal plane, in which their constituent notes form subordinate strands of melody.

Which of the two planes is perceived more vividly depends upon the style of the individual work.

CHAPTER V

The Concords of the Major Scale

IN the second chapter we saw that the source of consonance is the chord formed by a fundamental with its first five overtones.[1] Containing as it does two duplications of the fundamental—in our example, C—and one duplication of the second overtone —G—the chord can be thought of as in essence a three-note chord. For the purposes of analysis its chosen arrangement is its closest possible formation, i.e. with the fundamental C, forming

intervals of a major third with E, and of a fifth with G.

In this form the chord is called a common chord or, more technically, a major triad, the word triad expressing the fact that its constituent notes are three, and the word 'major' that its lower interval is a major third. It is all-important to observe that as well as upon the tonic itself of the major scale the chord can be built on two other of its notes. Thus in the scale of C,

the chord is available on the notes F and G .

Both these are, as it were, 'overtone chords': A and C are respectively F's fourth and second overtones, B and D respectively G's.

As less ideally concordant intervals are formed by inverting the natural positions of notes—thus, a minor sixth by inverting the more natural major third—so less ideally concordant major triads are formed. They have two so-called 'inversions', formed by either E or G usurping the position of the funda-

mental as bass note of the chord . Into the

different effect and use of these two inversions we need not

[1] See Example 8, page 11.

enter in this book: what we have to observe is the quality in common they have of undermining the sense of absolute repose of the natural chord in its root position (which, of course, is what one would expect). We shall see below how this undermining effect bears upon their relation to the logic of tonality.

The major triad and its two inversions form one group of concord. We must now consider the minor triad and its two inversions, which form the other group.

The minor triad has the same structure as the major one, with this momentous difference, that the major third between the fundamental and the fourth overtone is flattened to a minor third. In the familiar sad effect of the triad one can feel—so it seems to me—the power of the ideally consonant natural chord making itself felt in its absence. As we saw, in itself the minor third conveys no inherent effect of sadness; in itself it is a sensuously pleasing chord. The sadness which it conveys in this context seems to be the effect of an unconscious comparing of the minor triad to the major one, which it so resembles; of a feeling that the flattening of the overtone is a pathetic fall from the grace of the chord's natural state.

Whatever the cause, it is all-important to take note of the distinctive sadness of the minor triad. And to observe that in the major scale as there are three major, so there are three minor triads: in the scale of C they occur on the notes D, E and A: ♭ . F and A form intervals of a minor third and of a fifth respectively with D; G and B with E; and C and E with A.

Like the major triad, the minor triad gives rise to two inversions, built correspondingly, and having the same effect of undermining the repose of the triad in its root position.

* * * *

So much for our analysis. Before we close the laboratory door, let us arrange the various specimens of concord we have been considering in such a way that we can see, if as yet only dimly, their bearing upon the logic of tonality. Take a tune employing the notes of the major scale, with C as tonic. As this note is the focal point of the tune, so the major triad, to which in the major scale it acts as fundamental—the major triad, conveying a sense of ideal euphony and repose—is the focal point of the tune's harmonization. As in the tune each note, in virtue of the qualities of intervals, bears an individually significant relation to the tonic note, so in the harmonization each concord bears an individually significant relation to the major triad on the tonic. Thus the two inversions of this chord sound very 'like' the original, with the important difference that, the natural relation of fundamental and overtone being disturbed, they undermine its sense of repose. The two other major triads available in the scale, on F and G, also sound 'like' the tonic chord, but in an entirely different way: since they themselves are overtone-chords they convey the same sense of repose, but they do so *on different notes*: one might say that whereas the two inversions dilute the effect of the tonic chord, these other major triads obliterate and supplant it by an alternative, equivalent effect. So too, of course, do the respective inversions of these triads, except that here the effect is not equivalent, since being inversions, they lack repose. The three minor triads and their inversions also supplant the tonic chord, and here the effect is still less equivalent, since these minor triads differ from the tonic chord not only in that they are built on different notes, but in that the pattern of their structure is different. Their character, therefore, is different: the sense of repose, which in root position they convey and which their inversions undermine, is melancholy.

The various degrees of difference between all these chords and their focal point, the tonic chord, can be expressed in the following tabulation:

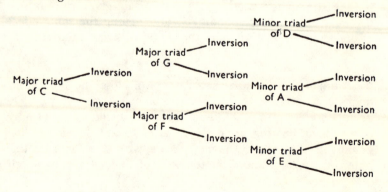

SUMMARY OF CHAPTER V

The concords of the major scale divide into four groups:

(1) The major triad, the ideally consonant overtone-chord, which conveys a sense of absolute repose. In the scale of C the chord can be built on C, the tonic, and on F and G.

(2) The inverted major triad in which one of the triad's other two notes usurps the position of the fundamental as bass note of the chord. This undermines the sense of absolute repose of the major triad in its root position.

(3) The minor triad which differs from the major triad in that the major third of the natural chord is flattened to a minor third. The minor triad also conveys an effect of repose, but its feeling is melancholy. It can be built on the D, E and A of the scale of C.

(4) The inverted minor triad which undermines the repose of the chord in its root position.

As in virtue of the qualities of intervals each note has a specific character in relation to the tonic, so in virtue of their different structure and position, each of these concords has a specific character in relation to the major triad on the tonic, which is the focal point of a tune's harmonization.

(1) The two inversions of the major triad on the tonic undermine its effect of repose.

(2) The two other available major triads convey the same effect of repose. But since these chords are not built upon the tonic this effect has the character of an alternative to that conveyed by the tonic's own major triad.

(3) The inversions of the two other major triads undermine their effect of repose.

(4) The three minor triads convey a repose which is not alternative to that of the major triad on the tonic, since the structure of the chord is different.

(5) The inversions of the three minor triads undermine their effect of repose.

CHAPTER VI

The Cadences and the Key System

HAVING analysed the individual concords we must now consider how they function at the cadences, which we have seen are the pivotal points of the logic of a melody.

Let us start by summarizing some general principles which in the light of our present knowledge we can assume must affect this functioning.

In the first place we can take for granted that, as the ear is 'selectively aware' of the relation between the final cadence-note and the tonic, notwithstanding the intervening notes, so it is 'selectively aware' of the relation between the final *chord* of a cadence and the chord of the tonic, notwithstanding the intervening chords. From this it follows that

(1) if the final chord of a cadence is the chord of the tonic there will be an effect of finality;

(2) if the final chord is an inversion of the chord of the tonic this effect of finality will be undermined;

(3) if the final chord is a chord other than that of the tonic the effect of finality will disappear and in its place will be an effect resembling it more or less, according to the nature of the chord: it will resemble it most if the chord is one of the two 'alternative equivalent' major triads, less if they are inverted, still less if the chord is a minor triad, least of all if it is an inverted minor triad.

The above concerns only the relation between the final chord of a cadence and that of the tonic. There remains to consider the chordal aspect of that other relation which we know affects the character of a cadence, namely, the character of the progression from the penultimate to the final note.

As to this, all that we can see at present is that the effect of the progression is likely to be influenced by the kind of intervals which the chordal progression will form below it. Thus if an upper interval pulls, its pull will be reinforced if lower intervals also do so, and weakened if they don't. Similarly if an upper interval moves 'reluctantly', its 'reluctance' will be greater if lower intervals do too; and on the other hand will be less if lower intervals pull. Precisely what the effect is when specific intervals combine in this way we cannot yet see; just this it is the purpose of this chapter to point out.

*   *   *   *

Thus introduced, the harmonic cadences present at first sight a frightening possibility of endless permutations and combinations. It is a relief to learn that in point of fact they crystallize into four and only four main types, each one of which is used so constantly that it is the custom in musical terminology to refer to the four as *the* cadences, as though between them they exhausted every cadential possibility. Nor is this by any means the only simplifying factor: all convey unmistakably specific effects, and have technical names which describe them; last, not least, these effects are interconnected.

The four cadences fall into two groups: in one are those whose final chord is that of the tonic; in the other in which it is some other chord. In a piece in C major (which I shall treat throughout this book as the prototype of the major scale) the first group consists of

> *The Perfect Cadence or Full Close*, in which the penultimate chord is the major triad of G and the final one the major triad of C;
>
> *The Plagal or Amen Cadence*,[1] in which the penultimate chord is the major triad of F and the final one the major triad of C.

The second group consists of

> *The Interrupted Cadence*, in which the penultimate chord is the major triad of G and the final chord variable;
>
> *The Imperfect Cadence or Half Close*, in which the penultimate chord is variable and the final one the major triad of G.

When the *penultimate* chord is an inversion, the cadence retains its specific effect and hence its name; but if the *final* chord is inverted the specific effect is so modified and undermined that the cadence has to be labelled 'inverted'. Thus a full close to an

---

[1] Since the term 'plagal', deriving from history, has no direct descriptive force, whereas the term 'amen' has (as we shall see), I will employ the latter in what follows.

inversion of the chord of the tonic is known as an 'inverted full close'.

Having thus introduced the cadences, let us proceed to consider them in detail, in the first place the full close and amen cadence to the chord of the tonic.

The first point to observe is that in both cadences the penultimate chord forms layers of pulling intervals with the final one. Thus in the full close the major triad of G supplies a rising semitone (B–C'), a falling tone (D'–C) and 'acoustic' fifths and fourths (G'–C, G–C'):

Ex. 22

- - - rising semitone

- - - - - falling tone
- - - - falling fifth
- - rising fourth

And in the amen cadence the major triad of F supplies a falling tone (A'–G), a falling semitone (F'–E) and 'acoustic' fifths and fourths (F–C', F'–C):

Ex. 23

- - - - falling tone
- - - falling semitone

- - - falling fourth
- - rising fifth

Our preliminary summary of general principles has prepared us for this; what it has not prepared us for—and this is the second (vitally important) point to be observed—is the striking difference of character of the two cadences. They are both equally final and yet there is no question that the approach from the major triad of G has a unique decisiveness, a masterful thrust, as of an arrow reaching its target, which more than earns the progression its titles of *perfect* cadence and *full* close; and that on the other hand in the approach from the major triad of F there is—in strongest possible contrast—a sense of lapsing upon the final chord rather than of thrusting to it, a sense of tranquil surrender, which makes it the ideal musical expression of the act of worship, from which it derives its name of amen cadence.

Since in this striking difference of character between these two cadences we are catching our first sight of a fact which can be regarded (in so far as any single fact can) as the core of the entire system of classical harmony it will repay us to examine it more closely and consider what might underlie it.

Two factors seem especially significant. In the first place, the full close contains, and the amen cadence does not, that progression to the tonic of a rising semitone, whose uniquely compelling pull we discussed at the close of the second chapter. Obviously this bears upon their difference of character.

The second factor, not quite so obvious, is the contrast between the intervals formed by the fundamentals of the two progressions, between the interval G–C' in the full close and F–C' in the amen. Both are acoustic intervals—the one a fourth, the other a fifth—conveying an effect of affinity, but there is this difference between them, that whereas in the former the C is the fundamental and the penultimate note, G, the overtone, in the latter this acoustic relation is reversed: C is now the overtone and the penultimate note, F, the fundamental.[1]

In our discussion of the 'acoustic intervals' we saw that the progression of overtone-to-fundamental conveys a more decisive pull than that of fundamental-to-overtone, since the fundamental, being the fundamental, exerts the stronger attraction. Evidently this has to do with the difference of character between the chordal progressions, based on these two pairs of notes, which we are considering. It is as though, in the full close, we feel the *chord* of C as the goal of the penultimate chord of G, its overtone—hence its masterful thrust. And hence the lapsing effect of the amen cadence: since the

---

[1] In the harmonic series of which F is the fundamental, C is the second overtone:

Ex. 24

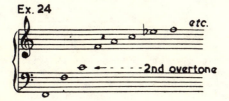

penultimate F is now the fundamental, the progression of its chord to the chord of C, its overtone, has the character of a lapse from a strong basic position to a weaker one.

Whatever the cause, the important point to observe is that of the two cadences the full close is the more decisive and, by reason of this greater decisiveness, the more significant. How significant is dramatically evident in the other two types of cadence, in each of which it is the major triad of G which functions—in the interrupted cadence as the penultimate chord, in the half close as the final one.

In the interrupted cadence the major triad of G is followed by some other chord than the chord of the tonic. So decisive is the thrust of the major triad to the chord of the tonic, so powerful the expectation that this is the chord that must follow it, that when this expectation is disappointed and another chord takes its place, the effect is precisely of an interruption—hence the name of the cadence. Here is an example of an interrupted cadence beside a full close:

Ex. 25

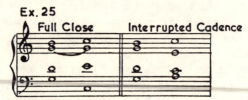

The second phrase of 'God save the Queen' contains an opportunity for an interrupted cadence. The melody here comes to rest upon the tonic; in itself, therefore, as I wrote in the first chapter, it conveys an effect of finality. Thus the harmony it calls for, one would think at first sight, is that of the full close:

Ex. 26

---

[1] The attentive reader will observe the omission of the fifth, G, from the final chord of this example. This omission is common practice. Since it is the fundamental's prominent second overtone the fifth is already sufficiently present in the chord; its absence lightens the sound without detracting from its essential quality.

But the third phrase—the phrase containing the cadence which, we saw, is the pivotal point of the whole tune—also calls for a full close. To have a full close immediately before this pivotal one would forestall and weaken its effect:

Ex. 27

Far better to treat the final C of the second phrase as pertaining not to the chord of the tonic, but to the minor triad of A, in fact to have an interrupted cadence. Instead of weakening we now strengthen the force of the pivotal full close: making good its previous interruption, reversing the false step it has just taken, the chord of G's progression to the tonic will bring an added power to the melody's logic:

Ex. 28

In the half close, in which the chord of G is now the final chord of a cadence, its pull to the chord of the tonic is operative in another way. What we have to bear in mind here is the fact that despite the intervening chords the ear is 'selectively aware' of the relation between the final chord of a cadence and the chord of the tonic. If the final D of the first phrase of 'God save the Queen' is harmonized as pertaining to the chord of G, the harmonization will destroy the sense which we saw the line of unaccompanied melody gives, of landing in a strange uncharted region; instead we shall feel—and this is where the pull of the chord is operative—that *the tonic is in the offing and that we know exactly where we are in relation to it.* Hence the name of half close. The 'half' has no mathematical significance: it is pictorial.

The conception of the cadence bearing to the full close the relation of a half to a whole depicts the effect the cadence conveys of moving to a point manifestly related to the chord of the tonic.

The chord of G as its final chord, conveying in virtue of its pull to the chord of the tonic an effect of 'halfness', is the constant feature of the half close; its variable feature is the penultimate chord. Often it is the minor triad on D:

Ex. 29

Dear | Harp of my | country in | darkness I | found thee

Equally often, perhaps even more so, the chord of the tonic itself:

Ex. 30

Way down upon the | Swanee river | far far a-way

Since G is C's second overtone, as C is F's, a half close taking this form is a sort of transposed amen cadence, coming to rest on G, instead of C. Thanks to it the chord of the tonic is able to do double duty in the cadences: not only in the full close to act as target of the thrusting chord of G, but *itself* lapse upon it.

I could write a great deal more about the half close—for example, about its other forms, involving other penultimate triads—and indeed about the other cadences, but I have written enough to achieve my present purpose, namely to show what the specific effects are which 'the' four harmonic cadences convey and, above all, in what ways they are interconnected. The connecting links, we can see, are the chord of the tonic, the chord of absolute finality, and the chord of the fifth note of the scale, G—the chord of the dominant, as this fifth note is aptly called—which in virtue of its dominion over the chord of the tonic, dominates the interrupted cadence and the half close. The system—one can call it that—can be roughly pictured in the following diagram:

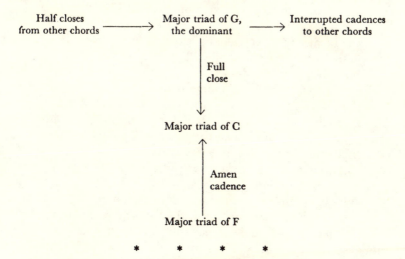

```
Half closes                    Major triad of G,              Interrupted cadences
from other chords   ────→         the dominant       ────→      to other chords

                                     Full
                                     close

                                       │
                                       ↓

                               Major triad of C

                                       ↑

                                     Amen
                                     cadence

                                       │

                               Major triad of F
```

*   *   *   *

In virtue of this system the logic of tonality acquires a quality of integration, immensely widening its scope—in short, the quality expressed by the word 'key'.

In the first chapter I compared the functioning of the tonic to the drawing of an 'invisible line' in relation to which other notes are 'placed'. Adhering to this image, one may say that when cadences are harnessed to the chordal progressions we have been studying the sense of an 'invisible line' is imprinted far more deeply. But not only this. Since within the framework of these chordal progressions each note of the major scale has its fixed specific place, the tonic's 'invisible line' becomes to all intents and purposes *the foundation-stone of a structure consisting of the scale's other notes*. All this is implicit in the word 'key' (not that the architectural image has any direct bearing on the etymology of the word[1]). As a building has a key-stone, so a key has a key-note, i.e. is the key *of* C or Bb or Gb. And as a key-stone is no key-stone until a structure which it supports

[1] The word derives from the Latin term 'clavis' for 'key' or 'lock', which in the Middle Ages was used by theorists in the sense of a 'note' or 'tone'.

begins to get built, so, until other notes are heard, a key-note is no key-note.

Because the other notes of a key function in specific ways, each has a specific nomenclature. Thus in the key of C major we have above the key-note or tonic, C,

the super-tonic, D;

the mediant, E—so called because it lies midway between the tonic and the dominant;

the sub-dominant, F—so called because it lies a fifth below the tonic, whereas the dominant lies a fifth above;

the dominant, G;

the sub-mediant, A—so called because it lies midway between the tonic and the sub-dominant;

the leading-note, B—so called because, being situated a semitone below the key-note, it forms a powerfully pulling progression 'leading' to it.[1]

So much for the new quality of integration (giving rise to these technicalities) which, I said, the key system brings to the logic of tonality. I added that this quality of integration immensely widens the scope of this logic. It does so because it carries with it the possibility of key change, the supreme resource of classical harmony. Concerning this I will pass a few preliminary remarks, before I conclude this chapter.

Because of this integration which the harmonic cadences bring, because of this deeply imprinted sense of a melody as a structure built upon the plane of its key-note, the ear is able to accept the plane of a given key-note as a point of departure to other melodies built upon the planes of other key-notes—in short, accept a change of key. Always provided that sooner or later the shift of plane is reversed and the original key restored in which the music can end as it began.

It will be seen that in essence this wider logic of key change is simply an expansion of the logic with which we are familiar. The chord of the tonic is now the key of the tonic; phrases cadencing to a final chord other than that of the tonic—to the chord of the dominant in the half close, of the sub-mediant in the interrupted cadence—are now whole sections cast in keys

[1] An alternative, less cumbrous—but also less descriptive—method of nomenclature is simply to number off the notes in roman numerals: thus the super-tonic is referred to as the II of a key, the mediant as the III, and so on.

other than that of the tonic; the phrase finally returning to the chord of the tonic is now a final section cast in the key of the tonic.

We must content ourselves here with this fleeting glimpse of the nature and underlying principle of key change. Before we can draw closer and study its actual workings we must do several things. We must first of all show how the minor scale, as well as the major, possesses the quality of being a key. We must then begin to increase our knowledge of the vocabulary of chords available within a key: from concords we must pass to discords; we must show how on the one hand discords bring variety and refinement to a melody cast in a single key, and how on the other hand they play a vital part in the process of key change itself.

The next chapters will accordingly be devoted to these topics.

SUMMARY OF CHAPTER VI

It is necessary to consider how concords function at the cadences, the pivotal points of a melody.

Their functioning can be considered from two points of view:

(1) The relation between the final chord of the cadence and the major triad on the tonic, which is the focal point of a melody's harmonization.

(The various forms which this relation can take have been discussed in the previous chapter.)

(2) The relation between the penultimate and the final chord of the cadence.

(It is the purpose of the present chapter to discuss the various forms which this relation can take.)

The penultimate and the final chord form four different types of cadence:

	Penultimate Chord	Final Chord
The perfect cadence or full close	major triad on G	major triad on C
The plagal or amen cadence	major triad on F	major triad on C
The interrupted cadence	major triad on G	variable
The imperfect cadence or half close	variable	major triad on G

There exists an important contrast of character between the full close and the amen cadence. The former thrusts decisively to the tonic triad; the latter lapses upon it. For this there are two reasons:

(1) The full close contains the progression of a rising semitone thrusting to the tonic.

(2) The progression of the roots, G and C, of the chords of the full close is that of an overtone to its fundamental; that of the roots F and C of the chords of the amen cadence, on the other hand, that of a fundamental to its overtone. (N.B.—C is F's second overtone.) Since an overtone-note pulls more powerfully to a fundamental than a fundamental to an overtone-note, the full close accordingly has the more decisive character.

The unique decisiveness of the full close is further reflected in the character of the interrupted cadence and in the half close.

The interrupted cadence owes its name to the fact that when instead of the major triad on C some other chord follows the major triad on G the effect is that of the interruption of an expected event.

The half close owes its name to the fact that, ending as it does on the major triad of G, it conveys the effect of movement to a point manifestly related to the chord of the tonic.

*   *   *   *

The four inter-related cadences impart to the logic of tonality the quality of integration expressed in the word 'key'. In the key system the tonic acts as the key-stone of a structure in which each note of the scale plays a specific harmonic role and bears a specific name.

The key system further contains the possibility of key change. A melody cast in a key imprints itself so deeply as a structure built upon the plane of its key-note that the ear is able to accept it as a point of departure to the planes of other key-notes. Ultimately, however, the ear demands that the music should return to its original key. Thus in essence key change is simply an extension of the elementary departure-in-order-to-return logic of tonality studied above.

CHAPTER VII

The Minor Key

My purpose in this chapter is to explain briefly the qualities which the minor scale shares with the major, in virtue of which it also is thought of as a key.

The two scales have the same history. Both occur among the twelve scales, the so-called Modes, established by the Church of the Middle Ages, each of the twelve being a different arrangement of tones and semitones within an octave. Since medieval theorists regarded the modes as of Greek origin they gave them Greek names: thus the major scale was called the Ionian and the minor the Aeolian mode. The Ionian was the only arrangement in which it was possible to build those major triads on the tonic, dominant, and sub-dominant, whose cadential functioning, conferring upon it the quality of a key, we described in the previous chapter. Hence the eclipse of the other modes after the close of the Middle Ages—of all save the Aeolian.

Not that this eclipse was deliberate, not that at a certain moment composers became alive to the superior possibilities of the Ionian mode and forthwith resolved to concentrate upon it: the process took place fortuitously, instinctively, without awareness of any ulterior consequence. Take for example the Mixolydian mode, which had every note in common with the Ionian save the flattened leading note (e.g. B♭ instead of B♮, if the tonic is C). When a piece of music in this mode cadenced to the tonic, composers instinctively sharpened the penultimate flattened leading note, in order to obtain a more decisive effect of finality, i.e. instinctively converted the reluctantly rising interval of a tone (B♭–C') into the urgently rising semitone (B♮–C'). Since the flattened leading note was the only feature which distinguished the Mixolydian from the Ionian mode, this practice of sharpening it at cadences led eventually to the extinction of the Mixolydian (until the twentieth century when composers in their search for an escape from the tyranny of the major-minor system revived it and the other modes; but that is another story).

It must now be explained why and in what form the Aeolian mode survived.

Like the Mixolydian, the Aeolian mode contained a flattened leading note; but as well it contained a flattened sub-mediant (A♭) and mediant (E♭). The practice of sharpening the leading note brought with it the practice of sharpening the sub-mediant too. In a phrase proceeding up the steps of the scale to a cadence on the tonic—thus, G, A♭, B♮, C—the A♭ produced in the context an uncomfortably wide interval with the B♮: instinctively composers hit upon the solution of closing the gap and rendering the melody smooth and even by sharpening the offending A♭. This brought the mode very near the Ionian, but it did not lead to its eclipse. In the first place the Aeolian contained (as the Mixolydian did not) another distinctive note, a flattened mediant, which the practice of cadential sharpening left intact. In the second place—and this is equally true of the Mixolydian and for that matter of the other modes—the practice of sharpening only occurred in a specific, albeit very frequent, context, that of a phrase *ascending* to a cadence on the tonic. Elsewhere the A♭ and B♭ of the Aeolian could be and were left intact. Thus the mode survived in two versions: a descending one, in which its original three flattened notes were preserved, and an ascending one, in which the A♭ and B♭ were sharpened. It was by utilizing notes from *both* versions that it proved possible to build a system of harmonic cadences equivalent to those of the major scale, imparting a sense of key.

Let us set forth the triads available in the two versions:[1]

Ex. 31

[1] The scale does not allow the building of either a major or a minor triad on the notes which I have placed between brackets.

The first—and most important—point to observe is that in the ascending version, thanks to the sharpened leading note, B♮, it is possible to build, as in the major scale, a major triad on the fifth note. If this chord should dominate a minor triad on the tonic as we have seen it do a major one, if it should pull to it with the same effect of decisive finality, then at once we begin to see why the minor should share with the major scale the quality of being a key.

In fact the chord does dominate a minor triad on the tonic. Nor is this surprising. We saw that a close affinity is felt between a major and a minor triad; that (so I suggested) the sadness of the minor triad is the effect of an unconscious comparing of it to the natural chord which it resembles, of a feeling that the flattening of the major third to a minor one is a 'pathetic fall from the grace of the chord's natural state'. Thus it is not surprising to find that a minor triad can take the place of a major one as the target of the chord of its second overtone, in other words that the major triad of G pulls as decisively to the minor triad as to the major triad of C.

From which it follows, then, that in the Aeolian mode it is possible to have a full close—and hence to have both an interrupted cadence, interrupting the pull of the full close by substituting another triad for that of the tonic, and a half close, in which the chord of the dominant at the end of a phrase, by reason of its pull to that of the tonic, gives a sense of manifest relation to it. Once again in fact we have a chord of the dominant working as the pivot of a system of interconnected cadences.

There remains to consider the Aeolian equivalent of the amen cadence, in which the chord of the dominant plays no part.

Here the case is not so simple. In the ascending version a major triad is available on the sub-dominant, as it is on the dominant, but its progression to a minor triad on the tonic does not at all correspond to its progression to a major one:

Ex. 32

. There is no sense of tranquil lapsing, but

on the contrary of discomfort. To attempt to account for this
would take us outside the scope of this chapter. We had better
just accept it, and also accept, without attempting to explain,
the fact that the situation can be saved and the progression
made to correspond to the amen cadence by the simple
expedient of converting the major triad on the sub-dominant
into the minor one available in the descending version of the

mode:
In this form the amen cadence

plays the same part in the minor key as it does in the major;
it provides an alternative to the full close sharply contrasting
with it.

Since in order to have a working system of harmonic cadences, in fact have a key, it is necessary to use both the sharpened leading note of the ascending version of the Aeolian (B♮)
and the flattened sub-mediant (A♭) of the descending version,
a so-called 'harmonic' minor scale was theoretically constructed
in the nineteenth century in which the different ascending and
descending versions were done away with and a flattened
sub-mediant and sharpened leading note retained as constant

features: . It is important to

bear in mind that this 'harmonic' minor scale *is* only a theoreti-
cal construction and that the true minor scale is the 'melodic'
minor, based on the two versions of the medieval Aeolian mode
—the 'melodic' minor being so called because, as we have seen,
it was originally for the sake of melodic effect that composers
took to sharpening the leading note and sub-mediant of the
ascending version. The 'melodic' minor is, I say, the true one,
since in practice the composers of the classical era have never
arbitrarily adhered to the A♭ and B♮ of the 'harmonic' minor;
whenever it has suited them they have taken advantage of the
wider resources of the 'melodic' minor and freely employed

the triads containing A♮'s and B♭'s. They have done so both within the body of the phrase and at the cadence. To attempt to explain here just how they have done this and with what consequences would be to involve myself prematurely in the topics of chromaticism and key change, with which I shall be dealing in subsequent chapters. I ask the reader, therefore, to let me leave the matter open at present—with the promise that the loose end will be tied up in due course later on.

SUMMARY OF CHAPTER VII

The purpose of this chapter is to show how the minor scale has the quality of a key.

The origin of the scale is the medieval Aeolian mode: C–D–E♭–F–G–A♭–B♭–C.

The practice arose of sharpening the B♭ in a phrase ascending to a cadence, and of sharpening the A♭ in order to narrow the interval to the sharpened B♭.

This practice left intact the descending version of the mode.

By utilizing notes of both versions it was possible to provide a system of interconnected cadences equivalent to those of the major key.

> The B♮ of the ascending version provided a chord of the dominant operative in the full close, interrupted cadence and half close.

> The A♭ of the descending version provided a chord of the sub-dominant operative in the amen cadence.

The structure of the modern *Harmonic* minor scale with its A♭ and B♮ reflects this development. Nevertheless the true minor scale is the *Melodic* scale with its two different versions, the descending one the original Aeolian mode and the ascending one the sharpened form of this mode. In practice composers have always exploited its wider resources and freely employed triads containing B♭'s and A♮'s. How they have done so will be explained later in this book.

CHAPTER VIII

The Formation of Discords

I will start this chapter by supposing that the reference just made to the use of chords of the 'melodic' minor scale 'both within the body of the phrase' and 'at the cadence' will have prompted the reader to voice a question for some time forming in his mind. 'Yes, indeed,' I imagine him exclaiming, 'what about harmony within the body of the phrase? So far you have been concentrating exclusively upon harmony at the cadences. Granted the importance of this, surely it is high time you began to deal with the harmony of the *whole* phrase? Surely to harp, as you have been doing, on the fact that the phrase moves to a goal is to overlook the truth that in music, as in other spheres of life, what matters is not only the goal, but the path by which it is reached?'

Such a question I would accept as a timely reminder. Let me at once begin to repair the omission complained of by supplying a harmonization of a phrase from the National Anthem. The harmonization must, of course, be kept within the limits of our present knowledge: must be strictly diatonic—i.e. confined to notes of a single key—and must consist exclusively of concords:

Ex. 35

long to— reign— over us

Compared to the familiar setting of the phrase heard every time we attend a theatre or cinema, that climactic chord under the word 'us' sounds distressingly thin as rendered here. Also the supporting voices lack rhythmic independence. They plod tamely along under the melody, adding absolutely nothing.

The fact of the matter is that the harmonization needs some touches of dissonance—which let us forthwith endeavour to supply. We shall, we know, have to bear in mind two considerations: on the one hand the vertical structure and character of the discord we produce, and on the other hand the horizontal intervals which its notes will form with those of the chords next door. Since as yet we have no idea of how to construct a discord vertically, we shall have to be content for the present to think horizontally. That is to say, we must regard the above harmonization as an adding to the tune of three lower melodies, and then set about improving these melodies in such a way that our improvement produces a telling dissonance. If this strikes the reader as a curiously roundabout method, then I would remind him that historically it was just this method which led to the creation of the classical discords. In the Church of the Renaissance, whose choral music was the source of the classical idiom, the attitude to harmony was primarily horizontal. The primary aim of the composer was to combine the simultaneous strands—the counterpoints—of melody which his choir would sing in such a way that each voice would set the others off and yet be individually beautiful. The discords which arose were not thought of as things-in-themselves to be labelled and analysed: they were offshoots of the counterpoint. Thus we are following in the wake of a distinguished precedent.

Let us concentrate on the first bar of our harmonization, in which the three lower voices are all tamely harnessed to the crotchet-followed-by-four-quavers rhythm of the tune. Since the crotchet of the first beat seems especially leaden-footed in comparison to the ensuing faster lighter quavers, let us give

our bass this dissonant quaver, B:  and

hope that its clash with the upper voices' E and C will prove acceptable.

It does—in fact it is hardly too much to say that the note transforms the effect of the whole bar. The question is, why?

Let us regard not the dissonance, but the new melodic line— C–B–A, instead of as before C–A—which we have given the bass. B and A form the descending interval of a tone, which, as we know, pulls; C and B form the still more strongly pulling interval of a descending semitone. Thus the progression C–B–A is forceful. Its forcefulness redeems the dissonance. Since we hear it as *occasioned* by the counterpoint of these powerfully pulling vocal intervals, the clash does not impinge as a chord in its own right; all we hear is a mere prickle, an agreeable one, ruffling the too smooth harmony of our diatonic concords.

Apart from this, the new note transforms the effect of the whole bar, because it alters its rhythm. Until now the tune has been tramping solidly forward in crotchets and occasional dotted crotchets. At last in this penultimate phrase it quickens into a succession of quavers—but only at the two latter 'weak' beats of the bar. Divide the first 'strong' beat also into quavers and we have the *whole* bar taking wing—doubling its pace as it approaches the last phrase, the climax of the tune.

It remains to add that melodically significant conjunct notes of lesser time value interpolated between the chords of a harmonization and clashing with them are known as *Inessential Notes*. When the interpolated note, as here, forms the figure of a scale with its neighbours it is known as a *Passing Note*. Other melodic figures which inessential notes can form (there are several others) it would be outside the scope of this chapter to describe.

*   *   *   *

Let us seek a further opportunity for successfully introducing a passing note into the National Anthem. On the face of it the second phase might seem to provide one:

Ex. 37

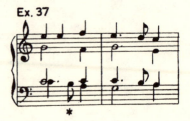

But no, this is not satisfactory. The presence of the solitary quaver so early in the tune, before its fundamental rhythm of crotchets has had time to establish itself, is irritating. Also we need a change of harmony at the 'weak' second beat of the first bar: the melody's two E's repeated above the sustained common chord of C sound dull and wooden.

Suppose now we take a step further and attempt to save the situation by lengthening the quaver into a crotchet and so converting the concord of the second beat into a discord:

Ex. 38

Certainly the effect is éxcellent. Lengthened into crotchets, the melodic counterpoint, C–B–A, which redeemed the dissonance of our quaver passing note, redeems the more drastic dissonance of the discord: more drastic, not only because held longer, but because, while the passing note clashed with voices which were being sustained, now the clash is produced by voices moving to a chord at the same instant. In fact we both have our cake and eat it: we keep our redeeming counterpoint—and indeed intensify its force, since B does not now drop lightly to A as it did when a mere passing note, but pushes its way down through the discord—and in keeping it create the change of harmony we need. A discord such as this one, falling on a 'weak' beat and interpolated between concords, is called a *Passing Chord*. The condition of its formation, namely, that it contains a note forming melodically forceful conjunct intervals with the notes of neighbouring chords, is the basic principle underlying the formation of classical discords generally.

*   *   *   *

Since our pursuit of dissonance is being conducted in the wake of the sixteenth century, let us take the following setting

of a psalter tune, composed in that period, for our next
example:[1]

Ex. 39

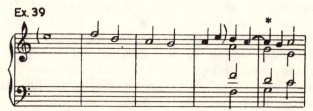

Here the discord is produced by a tie. The C on the last beat
of the penultimate bar, instead of proceeding directly to a B
on the first beat of the next bar, thus:

Ex. 40

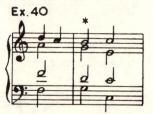

ousts the B and so doing converts what would otherwise have
been the consonant harmony of a major triad (B–D–G) into
a discord (C–D–G).

Evidently this is an even more drastic discord than the
passing chord of our previous example: whereas the latter fell
on a 'weak' beat and hence gave the effect of occurring *en route*
from one concord to another, here the discord takes the place
of a concord on a 'strong' beat—and a cadential concord at
that. On the other hand the voices do not move together, as
they did to the passing chord: the dissonant C is tied over from
a previous concord, i.e. is *prepared* (to use the technical expression). Furthermore the tension of the discord, like that of the
passing chord, is *resolved* (again the technical expression) in that
(i) it at once gives way to a concord, and (ii) the melodic pull
of a conjunct interval carries the ear forcefully from the
discord to the concord.

Actually, of course, the effect is delightful—indeed once
again it is a case of having our cake and eating it too. Not only

[1] By Louis Bourgeois (*c.* 1510-after 1561), quoted in *Historical Anthology of
Music*, ed. Davison and Apel, p. 144. I have rendered it here in the key of C,
instead of the original F.

does the tying of the C produce an interesting discord; it syncopates the rhythm, i.e. deprives a 'strong' beat of its expected accent. Deprived of this accent we are forced to imagine it; thus the deprival (and herein lies the peculiar charm of syncopation) has the paradoxical effect of compelling us to 'feel' the missing accent—and of course the discord falling upon it—more keenly through its very absence. Last, not least, the melodic force of the resolution brings an element of variety to the structure of the phrase. Just before the cadence there is a diversion; the phrase is, as it were, turning aside momentarily to reach a subordinate goal: the B on which the dissonant C must resolve. Thus its course is not, as but for the discord it would have been, a smooth and uninterrupted one.

A discord of this type, created by the holding over of a note from a previous concord, is called a *suspension*. Other forms of it were used in the sixteenth century, some of which must be illustrated here. Thus the suspension could be made by a lower

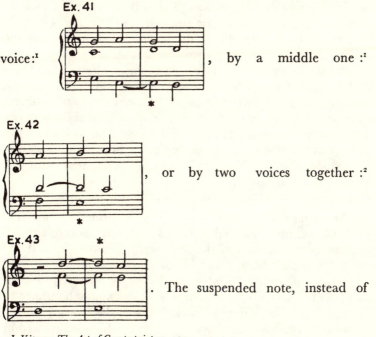

voice:[1]   , by a middle one :[1]

, or by two voices together :[2]

. The suspended note, instead of

---

[1] Kitson, *The Art of Counterpoint*, p. 134.
[2] ibid., p. 185.

moving directly to the note of resolution, could make a detour
through a melodically effective inessential note:

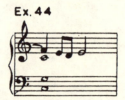

Ex. 44

Again, beneath the passage of the resolution the other voices,
instead of standing still, could move to form another concord:[1]

Ex. 45

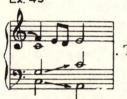

. These two latter forms contained the seeds

of far-reaching developments. In that it is making a melodic
detour, the dissonance of the suspended note is being thrown
into relief: here in embryo is the technique of protracting and
elaborating the resolution of discords which, as we shall see,
was to play so great a part in the classical idiom, reaching a
climax in the romantic harmony of the nineteenth century.
And in that a suspension is being followed by a *new* concord,
in that its resolution is not merely restoring the harmonic
status quo, which its dissonance has disturbed, but is leading to a
change of harmony, we can see a discord beginning to acquire
independence—and this tendency, too, increased with the
passing of the centuries.

*   *   *   *

The suspension and the passing note were the staple forms of
sixteenth-century dissonance. It was not until the revolt which
took place at the turn of the seventeenth century against the
refined complex polyphonic idiom of the Church, not until
the establishment of a cruder, secular art of opera and instrumental music, in which chords were used homophonically to
accompany a single line of melody, that the discord proper
came to be generally employed, i.e. the full-blooded discord in

[1] Kitson, *The Art of Counterpoint*, p. 137.

the modern sense of the term, of which the impact is not cushioned by a voice held over from a previous concord, but which all its constituent voices move to at the same moment.

One type of such discord we have already met in the passing chord, described above. Another type derives from the suspension. Suppose the dissonant C of the suspension of the psalter tune quoted above, instead of being 'prepared' by another C immediately in front, had been jumped to from some other

note, say A:
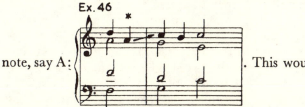
. This would produce

a discord in the modern sense of the term and furthermore, since it is falling on a 'strong' beat, a much more cogent and obtrusive one than a passing chord.

An infinitely more telling example of this type of discord is provided by the following phrase from the latter part of the slow movement of the 'Eroica':

The scale of demi-semi-quavers instead of going to a concordant A♭, as it did earlier in the movement:

now goes to a dissonant B♭, which then resolves on the A♭. Whoever has heard that phrase worthily performed will recall the eloquent beauty of that B♭. The sudden obtrusiveness of the unprepared suspension creates a need for resolution so urgent that the B♭ and its resolving A♭ almost for the moment seem to be coalescing into a separate melodic figure. The pull of B♭ to A♭—the 'psycho-physiological' pull of the falling tone—is here expressing pathos: the B♭, as though yearning to put an end to the dissonance which it has created, leans towards the note of its resolution. It is just this expressive leaning effect which the Italian name of *appoggiatura*, usually accorded to the unprepared suspension, describes. The verb 'appoggiare', from which it derives, means 'to lean'.

Not until we have further explored the subject of dissonance will we be able to gain an idea of the great range and significance of the unprepared suspension ('the history of music is written in the appoggiatura', it has been said, and the saying is not misleading). But already we are in a position to survey some of the forms it took. Thus, like the suspension, the appoggiatura could be executed by a lower or middle voice, or by two voices; it could make a melodic detour to the note of resolution; it could move to a new resolving concord. An eloquent example of a two-voiced appoggiatura is the opening phrase of the chorus 'Oh grief! His tortur'd heart' in the *St Matthew Passion*, in which the E♮ and the G are both clashing with the bass's F and then resolving:

Ex. 49

Bach's sacred music contains many an example of this heavily charged double appoggiatura (as it is called). No composer understood as he did its power to convey the depths of religious feeling, to express the sense of a crushing load of grief supported and transcended by faith. Into that brief quotation from 'Oh grief! His tortur'd heart'—so it seems to me—the very essence of the *St Matthew Passion* is distilled.

*   *   *   *

There remains finally to mention one other factor responsible for the formation of discords, one different in kind from those discussed above. This is the device of the 'pedal', deriving not from the sixteenth century, but rooted in the primitive beginnings of harmony. A pedal is a note—usually a bass note—sustained throughout a chordal passage regardless of the dissonances thereby formed:[1]

Ex. 50

On the face of it the device seems innocuous enough. The tonic pedal of the above example (most often the pedal is the tonic) converts concords into discords, yet somehow it leaves intact the individual character of each chord. Not that its effect is negligible: the continuous holding of the tonic weakens the momentum of the melody and of its supporting harmonies. That first phrase of the National Anthem now moves to its D, as it were, only with one foot, the other being tethered to the tonic. The tonic's 'invisible line'—to revert to my former metaphor—has been made visible and this has weakened that sense of departure, in which, as we have seen, lies the whole gist of the logic of tonality.

Why the device nevertheless survived and what important possibilities it contained we shall discover later. Together with the appoggiatura it played a part in the transformation and eventual disruption of the classical system. But it had also had an important share in the re-building which took place in the twentieth century.

SUMMARY OF CHAPTER VIII

The purpose of the chapter is to show how dissonance is produced horizontally.

---

[1] When not in the bass the pedal is called an 'inverted pedal'.

The following types of dissonance are distinguished:

(1) *The Passing Note*

Definition: an interpolated note of lesser time-value forming the figure of a scale with bordering notes.

A passing note produces a dissonance with a concord sustained through its passage.

The dissonance is redeemed by the melodic pull of the intervals which it forms and by the rhythmic variety which it introduces.

(2) *The Passing Chord*

Definition: an interpolated discord, usually occurring on a 'weak' beat, one of whose notes forms the figure of a scale with bordering notes.

The discord, since it is produced by voices moving to a chord at the same instant, is more drastic than the dissonance of the passing note.

Like the passing note, the passing chord is redeemed by the melodic pull of the intervals which it forms with bordering notes.

(3) *The Suspension*

Definition: a discord produced by the tying over of one of its notes from a preceding concord and resolved melodically by the tied note moving to a bordering note.

Although not produced by the simultaneous movement of voices, the suspension is more drastic than the passing chord since (a) it falls on a 'strong' beat and (b) the syncopation of the tied note enhances the effect of the 'strong' beat's accent.

Types of Suspension:

(a) a suspension can be made not only by an upper voice but by a lower or middle one, or by two voices;

(b) a suspended note, instead of moving directly to its note of resolution, can make a detour through a melodically effective inessential note;

(c) beneath the passage of the resolution the other voices instead of standing still can move to form another concord.

(4) *The Unprepared Suspension or Appoggiatura*

Definition: the suspension is 'unprepared' in that not only is its dissonant note untied, but it is preceded by a note of different pitch.[1]

---

[1] If the untied preceding note is of the same pitch, then the suspension is still technically regarded as 'prepared' and accordingly labelled a suspension—although, of course, the removal of the tie profoundly modifies its character.

Like the passing chord, the unprepared suspension is taken by voices simultaneously, but since it falls upon a 'strong' beat it is still more cogent. Furthermore, the unprepared dissonant note leans expressively to its note of resolution—hence the name, appoggiatura.

Types of Appoggiatura:
Like the suspension the appoggiatura can be executed by a lower or middle voice, by two voices, by a voice making a melodic detour to its note of resolution and by a voice beneath the passage of whose resolution the other voices, instead of standing still, form another concord.

(5) *The Pedal*
Definition: a note, usually the bass, sustained throughout a passage.

A sustained note converts what would otherwise have been concords into discords. When, as most often happens, the note is the tonic their consonant character is not destroyed. Not that the effect of the pedal is negligible: the continuous holding of the tonic weakens the momentum of the melody and of its supporting harmonies.

CHAPTER IX

The Dominant Seventh and the Process of Key Change

In the previous chapter we were not concerned with the structure of the discords which we formed. We did not lay them out on the laboratory table and inspect their anatomy, but studied them functioning organically in the context of live music. In this chapter we shall have to re-enter the laboratory for a while in order to inspect the structure of a discord of unique and vital importance, the so-called *Dominant Seventh*.

The dominant seventh is a chord of four notes, consisting of a major triad plus the note which forms with the root of the triad a minor seventh—thus the triad, C–E–G plus B♭. Such a chord is called a seventh because the interval between C, the root of the triad, and the B♭ is a minor seventh. Why it is called a *dominant* seventh we shall see later.

That the structure of the chord is a highly significant one the following two observations will reveal. First, if we turn to the table of the Harmonic Series given on page 10 and climb the ladder of C's overtones beyond the first five, which form the major triad, we find that the sixth overtone is B♭. Actually the overtone is a shade flatter than the corresponding note of the scale: it is, as it were, B♭ minus a barely perceptible quality.

Secondly, the sound of the chord C–E–G–B♭, although certainly that of a discord in the sense that it leaves the ear dissatisfied and demanding a concord to follow it, is nevertheless harmonious—indeed so much so that we can postpone its resolution in order to enjoy the luxury of dwelling upon it for its own sweet sake. And this harmoniousness, although impaired, also characterizes the chord's three inversions of

E–G–B♭–C, G–B♭–C–E, and B♭–C–E–G:

Ex.51

Evidently there is a significant connexion between the near-correspondence of the chord's structure to that of the Harmonic Series and its harmoniousness.

Why the chord is called the *dominant* seventh is easily explained. If we try to form the chord with the notes of the major scale, we find that it can only be built upon one note, the dominant, G. It cannot be built upon the tonic since the fourth note is a B *flat*, i.e. a chromatic note outside the diatonic scale. Neither can it be built upon the sub-dominant, F: the fourth note would be an E♭. It cannot be built on D, E, A, or B, since these notes are not the roots of major triads. Thus the only possibility is the dominant:

Ex.52

*   *   *   *

Let us now leave the laboratory and observe the dominant seventh in action. For the time being our best course will be to ignore what we have just learnt, to revert to the strictly horizontal standpoint of our previous chapter, and, with an open mind as to the kind of discord we shall produce, resume the task of adding helpful touches of dissonance to the diatonic concords of a harmonization of the National Anthem.

For example, take the full close of the final phrase:

Ex.53

Knowing as we do how cogently final the full close is, at first sight it seems rank impertinence to single one out for improvement. If, however, we overcome our awe of the full close and look without prejudice at the horizontal movement of the voices we shall see that—full close or no full close—the line of the alto could undoubtedly be improved if we were to

convert its last three notes, G–G–E, into the melodically much
more forceful scale, G–F–E:

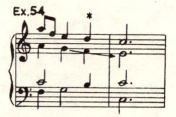

By doing this we convert the dominant triad of our full close
into a passing chord, the passing chord here being G–B–D–F,
the chord of the dominant seventh.

If the reader will compare our original harmonization of the
phrase with this one, he will agree that the effect of the dominant seventh is admirable. The addition of the dominant's sixth
overtone-note, F, pulling as it does powerfully down a semitone
to the E of the tonic chord, far from blunting the thrust of the
dominant chord, only serves to make it more forceful: indeed,
one can say that as a result of the alteration *the full close is still a
full close, only now fuller than ever.*

In fact it comes to this, that the chord of the dominant
seventh can take the place of the simple chord of the dominant
in the pivotal cadence of the key system. In taking its place it
does not oust it—the dominant seventh contains the chord of
the dominant—but reinforces it: through the four-note discord
the three-note triad is still operative, but now even more
vigorously and powerfully. It is as though Nature, not content
with furnishing the ideally consonant major triad, had gone
further and supplied the potential dynamic of a system. *In itself*
the chord of the dominant is not dynamic; it is a reposeful
concord, whose thrust to the chord of the tonic is only felt
when the latter is joined to it. Convert the dominant chord into
a dissonant dominant seventh demanding the tonic to resolve
it, and its potential thrust becomes an actual one, becomes a
thrust *felt in the very sound of the chord.*

It remains to add that a dominant seventh is also available
on the dominant of the 'harmonic' minor scale and that the
thrust of the seventh reinforces the full close of a minor key as
it does that of a major one.

*   *   *   *

Now that we understand the structure and functioning of the dominant seventh we are at last able to broaden our field of vision, to pass beyond the narrow orbit of the melody cast in a single key and consider the nature of key change, that supreme resource of classical harmony, through which the logic of tonality finds its fullest scope.

A change of key is felt to take place when

(1) a note not belonging to the prevailing key is introduced;

(2) this note is followed by another note or notes with which it belongs in another key.

Thus the first phrase of 'O God our help in ages past' is in

Ex. 55

C major:  . The second

phrase contains an F♯, a note not belonging to C major:

Ex. 56

 . The F♯ is followed by G,

a note with which it belongs in the key of G major; it is indeed the leading note of that key. In the context the F♯ destroys G's character as the dominant of C major and gives it instead that of the tonic of G major; in other words it changes the key.

The harmony implied by the progression of leading note to tonic of a new key is that of the dominant-to-tonic full close, the full close now taking place in the new key. The chord of the new dominant could be the simple major triad:

Ex. 57

but its potency as a key-changing chord will be greater if it is converted into a thrusting dominant seventh:

Ex.58

Indeed, so powerful is the thrust that the mere sound of the dominant seventh of a new key tends to disrupt the old key and create the effect of *already* being in a new one. When, as in the above example, the new dominant seventh is at once followed by the tonic to which it thrusts, the feeling is borne out; to put it technically the new key is *established.* In an extended work it is by thus exploiting the thrust of the dominant seventh that key changes are most usually effected.[1]

We must now consider another factor in the process of key change: modulation. 'Modulation', writes Dr Scholes in the *Oxford Companion,* 'may be familiarly defined as a method of key change without pain.' A key change may cause 'pain', because in the nature of the case the new dominant chord[2] contains a chromatic note not belonging to the original key: at the moment of its impact, therefore, its tendency is, as I remarked above, to disrupt—hence the 'pain'. (Not that a disrupting effect is necessarily always painful; after a surfeit of diatonic harmony an unexpected chromaticism can on the contrary be welcome, a refreshing stroke of colour relieving a dull view—indeed the very word 'chromatic', derived from the Greek word 'khroma' meaning colour, implies this.)

The method of modulation, which gets rid of the disrupting effect, is so to arrange the succession of chords that the dominant chord[2] of the new key *is immediately preceded by a chord which the new key and the old have in common.* Suppose, for example, we were to place an inverted minor triad of A, which occurs in G major as well as in C major, immediately in front of the

---

[1] Because the dominant seventh conveys a powerful thrust it does not follow that its effect in any context is necessarily one of power. Often the reverse is true. Just because *qua* chord it is so highly charged, if used indiscriminately it creates an effect of exaggeration and sentimentality. Thus it would be overdoing it to put a dominant seventh under the F♯ of the second phrase of 'O God our help', quoted above. The sheer force of its thrust to a new key would do violence to the structure of the brief simple melody.

[2] i.e. the dominant triad or dominant seventh, as the case may be.

G major dominant triad of our 'O God our help' example:

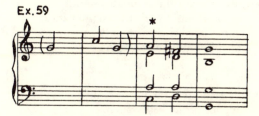

Ex. 59

In the context the inverted triad acts like a hinge: it switches us from the track of C on which it lies, and along which we approach it, to the track of G on which it *also* lies. 'Pain' is eliminated because we do not jump the rails, because, thanks to the railway-point of the modulating triad, we pass imperceptibly from one key to the other. Had the triad been, say, the major triad of F, which does *not* occur in G major:

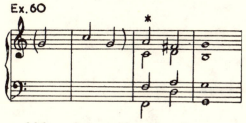

Ex. 60

the bump would have been noticeable.

       *   *   *   *

These processes of key change, i.e. the introduction of the new key by the sounding of its dominant triad or dominant seventh followed by its tonic, and the employment—or not, as the case may be—of a preliminary modulating chord, are *constant* elements of key change, are, so to speak, mechanisms by means of which changes of key are operated. Apart from them a number of *variable* factors of cardinal importance are involved, with which I must now deal in the chapters to come.

SUMMARY OF CHAPTER IX

The structure of the dominant seventh

The dominant seventh is a four-note discord, consisting of a major triad plus the note which forms with the root of the triad the interval of a minor seventh, thus C–E–G–B♭.

The fact that B♭ is C's sixth overtone, and that, although a discord, the chord is harmonious, indicates that like the major triad, the chord has an acoustic significance.

In the major scale the chord can only be built on G, the dominant. Hence its name of 'dominant seventh'.

The functioning of the dominant seventh

It powerfully reinforces the triad of the dominant in the full close, the pivotal cadence of the key system.

(1) F, the note which forms with G the interval of a minor seventh, pulls powerfully to the E of the tonic chord.

(2) Whereas the dominant triad is a reposeful concord the dominant seventh is a discord demanding resolution.

The dominant seventh can also be built on the dominant of the 'harmonic' minor scale and functions in the minor key as in the major one.

*   *   *   *

The structure and functioning of the dominant seventh understood, the nature of key change, the supreme resource of classical harmony, can be investigated.

The nature of key change

A key change takes place when a note not belonging to the prevailing key is introduced, followed by another note with which it belongs in another key. Thus F♯ introduced into a melody in C major and followed by G, would effect a change to the key of G major.

The harmony implied by the progression F♯-G is that of a full close, the full close taking place in the new key.

If the dominant triad of the full close is converted into a dominant seventh the new key is said to be 'established'. In an extended work the normal method of 'establishing' a new key is by this use of the dominant seventh.

The nature of modulation

Modulation is a method of smoothing the passage to the new key by placing immediately in front of its dominant chord, which is chromatic to the original key and therefore disrupting in its effect, a chord which the original and the new key have in common.

CHAPTER X

Key Change to 'Related' Keys

THE variable factors involved in a change of key are of two kinds:

    (1) the choice of new key;
    (2) the structural function of the key change.

In what follows I shall deal first with the latter of these factors. Regarding the former, all that need be said at present is that 'new' keys fall into two classes, those which are *related* to the old key (hence the title of this chapter) and those which are *remote* from it. The technical meaning of the terms *related* and *remote* will be explained in due course.

By the 'structural function' of a key change I mean the part which it plays *in the context of a given piece*. Take for example the case—which we have not yet met—of a key change occurring not at the end of a phrase, as in 'O God our help', but *within* the phrase—as in the following quotation from 'Early One Morning':

Ex. 61

"... I heard a maid sing in the vall - ey be - low "

The alto's chromatic B♭ beneath the 'the' of the second bar converts the inverted major triad of C, which the other voices are forming, into an inverted dominant seventh of the key of F major. Since the new dominant seventh is duly followed by the tonic to which it thrusts it brings about a change of key.

It brings about a change of key, but—and the 'but' is a very big one—an extremely brief insignificant change, since the new key is no sooner 'established' than the phrase executes a full close back into the original key. Indeed so insignificant is the effect that such a change is not reckoned as a key change proper but classed as a separate type, the so-called *passing* or *ornamental* key change.

And yet, for all its insignificance *qua* key change, the passing change does perform a structural function. Consider that 'Early One Morning' example again. The chromatic dominant seventh is, we can see, a passing chord, the alto taking the B♭ on the way down from C to A. Imagine now the effect of the progression if the passing chord, like those which we created above, had been a diatonic one, i.e. if the B♭ had been a B♮:

Ex. 62

There is no question that the B♭ has a much greater force, that the pathetic inflexion of the falling semitone, B♭–A, together with the fact that the chromatic passing chord, created by the B♭, is the dominant seventh of A's chord, bring a more powerful element of variety to the internal structure of the phrase than the merely diatonic passing chord.

Let us now deal with the type of change represented by our 'O God our Help' example, a cadential change occurring at the end of a phrase. Since, as we know, the final note of a phrase is felt as its goal the sense of a change of key is definitive when the final chord is a new tonic—is definitive even though the change may last no longer than the mere sounding of the new tonic, even though the music at once turns back to the old key.

Just *how* definitive, however, depends on the context, i.e. upon the place which the full close into the new key occupies in the melodic scheme of the piece as a whole. In 'O God our Help' the change to the key of G occurs in the middle of the

tune, and is its central pivotal point: the first two phrases end
in a movement away from the original key, the second two in a
corresponding movement back to it:

Ex. 63

Now compare this to the following change which we could
introduce into the second phrase of the National Anthem (it is,
as a matter of fact, the stock harmonization):

Ex. 64

Whereas before we had an interrupted cadence (see page 37),
now by sharpening the bass's G we have a change to the key
of A minor (instead of the triad of the dominant as penultimate
chord, we have an inversion of the dominant seventh of
A minor, E–G♯–B–D). In itself the change, occurring as it does
at the end of the phrase, is definitive but since the pivotal point
of the tune is not here but at the full close of the third phrase
(that full close reaffirming the tonic 'in view of the excursions
to come', as I put it), its impact is not to be compared to that
of the change in 'O God our Help'. The new dominant seventh
brings the A minor chord into sharper focus—but it could be
dispensed with without any damage to the structure of the tune.
The interrupted cadence of our original harmonization was
perfectly satisfactory.

Let us now take the case of a change to a key that is adhered
to. 'Where the Bee sucks' will serve as our example:

Ex. 65

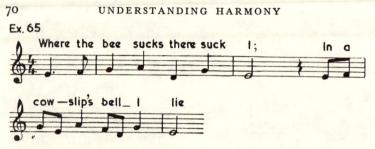

After these two phrases in the home key the third phrase makes a 'passing' change and finally a full close into the key of its dominant, G, a key which will in the following phrases be adhered to:

Ex. 66

Then follows the passage in the new key:

Ex. 67

Almost immediately (to be precise, in the second bar where the F♯ of G major is converted back into a natural) the piece returns to the home key in which it ends:

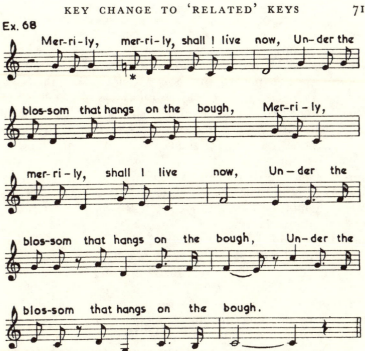

The structure of this much longer piece is quite different from that of 'O God our Help', and the difference has everything to do with the fact that the new key is adhered to. 'O God our Help', moving away from the home key and then back again, is a two-part, *binary* structure; 'Where the Bee sucks' a three-part *ternary* one. The first part ends with the full close in the new key; the second part adheres to the new key; the third part returns home. The fact that the second part *remains* in the new key, that the new camp is not raised at once, but made to serve as the base of further operations, is the *sine qua non* of the ternary structure. The G major flight of quavers of 'On the bat's back I do fly' would lose their momentum if they were cast in the home key of C major: instead of flying further afield we should feel that we were laboriously setting out all over again. And the third part in which the home key is so charmingly restored would have no point, since, the key never having been departed from, there would be nothing to restore.

In this analysis we are catching our first sight of a fact of far-reaching consequence, a fact to which is due the whole possibility of using the device of key change as a method of large-scale construction. I said that in the third part the home key is *restored*. That we feel its return to be a restoration means that, superseded though it has been by another key, the home key has not been forgotten, that its imprint is still fresh in our mind. We never cease to be aware that the new tonic, for all the fact that it is a tonic, is a *new* one. Not only that, we never cease to be aware of the original relation of the new tonic to the old one, to be aware that the G major triad of the second part was once the dominant chord of C major, and *never cease to demand that sooner or later it shall be again*. Thus when, instead of merely moving out of his home key, the composer *stays* out, he can still employ the basic depart-in-order-to-return principle of tonality, but on a new and much larger scale. The sixteen bars of 'O God our Help' do not allow of more than a brief touching of a new key; 'Where the Bee sucks' provides a much more complete escape from the yoke of the original tonic and for this very reason (since the more complete the escape from the tonic the greater the effect of its restoration) more elbow-room in which to expand the passage of its return.

'Where the Bee sucks' raises one more issue which I must briefly touch upon. It concerns the passing change and the full close into the key of G occurring in the third phrase:

Ex. 69

Since here the new key is going to be adhered to these two changes cannot be dismissed as belonging to the same category as the at first sight similar examples we studied in 'Early One Morning' and 'O God our Help'. Their mechanism is the same, but *in this context* they function differently. In this context the harmonic inflexion of the 'passing' change and the full close establishing the new key at the end of the phrase have an extra significance: they turn out to be the preliminary stages of a process of suppressing the old key in favour of a new one. The phrase, setting out as it does from C, first glancing at G in the 'passing' change, and then ending in it, acts as a sort of bridge from the one key to the other; the 'passing' change, as it were, gives advance notice of the full close, and the full close of the section in the new key. Later in this book when we come to discuss the topic of sonata-form we shall see what an immensely important part 'bridge passages' such as this are capable of playing in a wider framework.

*   *   *   *

We must now turn to consider the other kind of variable factor involved in a change of key: the choice of new key.

New keys, I remarked, are classed as either *related* or *remote*. A related key, as we would expect, is one which has the maximum number of notes in common with the home key. C major's related keys are:

> The minor key of its super-tonic, D;
>
> The minor key of its mediant, E;
>
> The major key of its sub-dominant, F;
>
> The major key of its dominant, G;
>
> The minor key of its sub-mediant, A. This particular minor key, whose descending version has every note in common with C major, is known as 'the relative minor'.

C minor's related keys are:

> The major key of its mediant E♭, which, having every note in common with its descending version, is known as its 'relative major';
>
> The minor key of its sub-dominant, F;
>
> The minor key of its dominant, G;
>
> The major key of its sub-mediant, A♭;
>
> The major key of its flattened leading note, B♭.

It is important to observe that the tonic triads of all these related keys fall within the scale of the home key. Thus the tonic triads of F and G major and of D, E and A minor are all diatonic chords in the scale of C major:

Ex.70

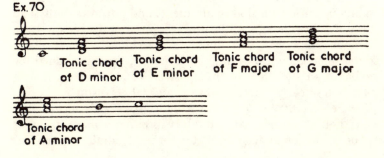

Tonic chord of D minor   Tonic chord of E minor   Tonic chord of F major   Tonic chord of G major

Tonic chord of A minor

Similarly the tonic triads of E♭, B♭, and A♭ major, and of F and G minor are diatonic in the melodic scale of C minor:

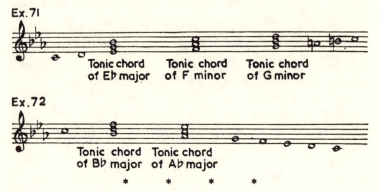

Ex. 71

Tonic chord of E♭ major   Tonic chord of F minor   Tonic chord of G minor

Ex. 72

Tonic chord of B♭ major   Tonic chord of A♭ major

*   *   *   *

From the beginning of the seventeenth century, when the major-minor system first began to take shape, until the period of Bach (1685–1750) and Handel (1685–1759) all key changes were normally confined to related keys. Partly the explanation for this is a technical one. For acoustic reasons, into which we need not enter, it is not possible on a keyboard instrument to have every one of the twenty-four available keys all equally in tune. Under the so-called 'Mean-Tone' system of keyboard temperament which prevailed in the seventeenth century the six major keys of B♭, F, C, G, D, and A and the three minor keys of G, D, and A were as good as perfectly in tune; all the others were perceptibly out. (Thus B♭ was in tune with the other notes of the key of B♭ major; but if B♭ were treated as an A♯ and used in the key of B minor—or some other key requiring an A♯—it would be jarringly out of tune.) Since most of the above-mentioned nine available keys are related in the sense defined above, i.e. have the maximum number of notes in common, this meant that to all intents and purposes the system precluded key changes to the great majority of the remote keys. In Bach's day this limitation was overcome by the brilliant contrivance known as 'Equal Temperament', which tuned the keyboard in such a way that, instead of as formerly having some notes nearly perfectly in tune and others disturbingly out, all were equally but only very slightly out: this meant that every note could now safely do duty as either a sharp or flat as the occasion demanded and that accordingly all the twenty-four keys were thrown open. It was to advocate this deliverance that Bach composed his most renowned instrumental work, the *Well-tempered Clavier*, consisting of two sets of twenty-four Preludes and Fugues, each cast in a different key.

But technicalities of keyboard tuning were not the only reason why the key changes of the period were normally confined to the 'related' keys. That they were not, the *Well-tempered Clavier* itself reveals: not one of the forty-eight Preludes and Fugues contains a 'remote' key change; in each Bach was content to remain strictly within the orbit of keys 'related' to his given key. This was not due to mere force of habit, but to a deeper reason, which we must now examine.

I pointed out during my examination of the structure of 'Where the Bee sucks' that, when a key changes, not only do we not forget the old tonic, but we never cease to be aware of the new one's original relation to it. There are, however, degrees of awareness and the fact is that if the new tonic was a diatonic chord in the home key—was the chord of its dominant or super-tonic or what have you—then not only do we continue to be aware of this, but *keenly, acutely aware*. The new tonic takes charge, acts as the centre of a new key, furnished with *its* dominant, subdominant, and other chords, yet still the place it occupied in the scheme of the original key is vivid in our minds. Because this is so, the structure of such a key change is easy to grasp, and therefore in the period we are considering, in which the major-minor system was first beginning to unfold its possibilities, key changes were normally confined to related keys. For in music, as in any other form of skill, the first stage of a development lies in the mastery of what is simple.

The examples of key change given in the early part of this chapter were all to related keys. Looking back upon them now we can see that while a development is well under way in 'Where the Bee sucks', with its whole middle section cast in a new key, in the others it has not gone very far. Despite the contrast, which I stressed, between the insignificance of the passing change in 'Early One Morning' and the definitiveness of the cadential change in 'O God our Help', the fact of the matter is (and I say this at the risk of seeming to contradict myself) that *because the new key is a related one* in neither case is there any real sense of departure from the old key. The old tonic is still dominating the stage and all that is happening is a temporary shift of spotlight to another chord—a spotlight which in the case of the passing change is a mere flicker across the face of the chord, but which in that of the cadential change comes to rest upon it, but only for an instant. Indeed one can roundly say of these brief changes to related keys that their function is not really to change key at all, but rather to expand the range of the original key. The dominant sevenths of the related keys are admitted not, as it were, in order to dethrone the original tonic, but in order to enable it from time to time to delegate its authority to one of the other potential tonic chords which the key contains.

This may seem arbitrary; perhaps it will seem less so when I point out that their preference for the related key change is one of the chief factors distinguishing Handel and Bach and their predecessors from later composers, and that in the case of Handel (less so in that of Bach in whose music other factors play a preponderant role) one can single out this one factor and claim that since usually his key changes have the character I have described, because his passing and cadential changes merely have the effect of expanding the range of a single key, and because when a change is adhered to the original relation between the old tonic and the new one can be so easily grasped, his idiom has that characteristic simplicity—that simplicity sometimes verging on dullness, but at other times (one thinks of the great choruses) a source of blazing power and splendour. And if the music of Handel's great successors on the whole lacks that Handelian simplicity, and if besides it is charged, more often than his, with dramatic tension, thrill, and mystery, one of the chief reasons is the development of the resource of the remote key change.

In conclusion I owe the reader a preliminary word regarding the remote key change. When the tonic chord of a new key is not diatonic in the old one, the relation between the two chords is less clearly grasped. This does not mean, however, that the tonic triad of a remote key, because it is chromatic, therefore necessarily occupies no place in the scheme of the home key. Certain chromatic triads occupy a very important place. This being so, we must for the time being turn aside from the subject of key change and in the next chapter discuss some of these chromatic triads and outline some of the principles of chromaticism. We shall then be able to resume the topic of key change and explore the far-reaching vistas which remote changes open up.

SUMMARY OF CHAPTER X

The 'establishing' of a new key by the employment of its dominant seventh in the full close with or without a preliminary modulating chord forms the mechanism by means of which key changes in general operate. The working of the mechanism is influenced by a number of variable factors of cardinal importance to be considered in the present and subsequent chapters. These are of two kinds:

(1) *The structural function of the key change*

Three types of key change can be distinguished according to their role within the structure of a piece:

(i) *The 'passing' or 'ornamental' key change*

A change occurring within the phrase followed immediately by a reversion to the original key.

The effect *qua* key change is insignificant. Nevertheless it brings variety to the internal structure of the phrase.

(ii) *The cadential key change*

A change occurring at the end of a phrase.

Since the last note of a phrase is felt as its goal the effect of the change is definitive even when immediately followed by a phrase reverting to the original key.

How definitive the effect is depends upon the part played by the full close in the melodic scheme of a piece. Thus in 'O God our Help' the change to the key of G major, occurring at the central pivotal point of the tune, is more definitive than the change to the key of A minor in the second phrase of the National Anthem.

(iii) *The key change followed by a passage in the new key*

Such a passage raises a demand for the restoration of the original key. Thus the 'depart-in-order-to-return' logic of tonality becomes the principle of an extended three-part 'ternary' structure, consisting of a section in the original key, a middle section in a new key, and a final section in the original key.

(2) *The choice of new key*

New keys are either related to or remote from the original key. A key's related keys are those which have the maximum number of notes in common with it. C major's related keys are D minor, E minor, F major, G major and A minor. C minor's are E♭ major, F minor, G minor, A♭ major, and B♭ major. The tonic chords of all these keys occur in the scales of C major and C minor respectively.

> From the beginning of the seventeenth century to the period of Bach and Handel key changes were normally confined to related keys. This was partly due to technicalities of tuning, but also to the fact that when the tonic of a new key occurs in the scale of the old one, the relationship between the two is experienced as obvious and intimate. So much so that brief passing and cadential changes to related keys convey no real sense of departure from the home key; rather their effect is to expand its range. The dominant sevenths of these keys do not impair the authority of the home key's tonic; by means of them its authority is temporarily delegated to one of the other potential tonics which the scale contains.

The remote keys are less obviously and intimately related to the home key, since their tonic triads do not occur within its scale, but are chromatic. Before the topic of key change can be resumed it is necessary in the next chapter to outline some of the principles of chromaticism and also to discuss the part which chromatic triads play in the scheme of a key.

CHAPTER XI

Chromatic Triads

HITHERTO our chief example of a chord chromatic to a key has been the dominant seventh of a new key in the context of a key change. Since here in the act of disrupting the old key the chord is setting up a new one, this is in the nature of a special case: the dominant seventh is chromatic to the old key, but in the new one to which it leads it is diatonic; as the succinct technical phrase puts it, it is *approached chromatically* and *quitted diatonically*. Whereas the triads which we are about to consider are *both approached and quitted chromatically*. This time, when we leave the road of a key we are not going to be re-routed; we are going to be pushed right off the highway into a trackless field.

At first sight one might think that the key system, based as it is on a relation of specific notes to a central tonic, could not tolerate such rough handling, that it would be shaken to its very foundations if a disrupting chromatic chord did not at once justify its intrusion by leading straightway to another key. The truth is that the system could easily tolerate the intrusion, and furthermore that, to become an artistic medium capable of expressing the gamut of human feeling, it needed to be able to make room for just this incalculable abnormal disrupting element. We shall see below how in the romantic idiom of the nineteenth century chromaticism came to modify and transform the system, and how its disruptive tendency afterwards came to a head in the modern trend of atonality.

The key system, I said above, could *easily* tolerate chromaticism. It imposed the same terms upon which it admitted diatonic discords: as the diatonic dissonant note could justify its intrusion by functioning melodically as an inessential note or in a passing chord, suspension or appoggiatura, so a chromatic note could. Since every note of the diatonic scale is bordered by a chromatic note capable of pulling melodically to it either a semitone down or one up, this condition of entry could be easily met. Here, for example, is Mozart introducing a chromatic appoggiatura chord into Sarastro's great aria, 'In diesen heil' gen Hallen' in *The Magic Flute*:

Ex.73

The chromatic B♯ redeems its drastic clash with the inverted minor triad of F♯ by the melodic force of its movement to the C♯ semitone above.

Here again is Mendelssohn introducing a chromatic passing note D♯ into the opening phrase of the 'Spring Song':

Ex.74

In both the above examples the chromaticism produces a dissonance. Chromatic triads, with which we are here concerned, are subject to the same condition of entry: the chromatic note which builds them—the A♭ say, which combined with F and C would produce a chromatic minor instead of a diatonic major triad on the sub-dominant of C major—must function melodically. But the impact of a concordant triad is necessarily very different from that of a discord. Chromatic though it is, the triad is a stable reposeful chord carrying weight and drawing attention to itself. In our analysis of the diatonic triads of the major scale we saw that each is related to the chord of the tonic in an individually significant way: the same is true of chromatic triads. Many factors are involved, too complex to discuss in detail here: it will suffice if I point to a few of the most frequent important chords and if, in seeking to account

for their significance, I confine myself to causes lying readily
to hand. Such a chord, for example, is the major triad on the
super-tonic, e.g. in the key of C major, the major triad of D,
containing a chromatic F♯. Normally it resolves melodically on
the chord of the tonic, thus:

Ex. 75

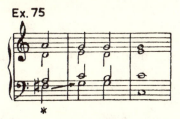

Since the time of Bach this chromatic triad has enjoyed the
privileged status of a naturalized foreigner in both a major and
a minor key. An explanation lying to hand and going far to
account for the effect which the foreign chord makes of being
at home in the key, is the fact that, as the technical phrase puts
it, the triad is built on 'the dominant of the dominant', e.g.
that it is built on the dominant, D, of C's dominant, G. It is as
though in this case the foreigner had acquired rights of natural-
ization by marrying into C's family.

Another chromatic triad demanding mention is that of the
flattened sub-mediant, e.g. in C major the major triad of A♭.
Here there is no question of a foreigner marrying into C's
family: the chord remains a stranger, and therein lies its virtue.
In the context of C major the foreigner has a sensuous charm,
its chromaticism shines with an exotic peacock brilliance. And
yet, for all its foreignness, it resolves effortlessly into the tonic
chord, melts into it, as though there were some affinity between
the two:

Ex. 76

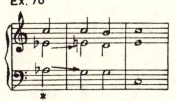

In point of fact there is some affinity: A♭, the root of the triad,
lies a major third below C, and the major third is *par excellence*
the sensuously pleasing consonant interval—hence (one is

tempted to presume) the sensuous charm of Ab's *triad* in the key of C and the effortlessness of its resolution. The chromatic major triad of E, C's mediant, whose root lies a major third above C, has a similar charm and its resolution a similar effortlessness. And since, as we saw, the interval of a minor third is also sensuously pleasing, so too have the chromatic triads whose roots lie respectively a minor third below and above the tonic, e.g. in C major the major triads of A and Eb. In fact these chromatic triads with roots an interval of a third from the tonic form something of a class apart—an important class, as we shall see when we come to consider the topic of remote key change.

Another fascinating foreigner is the so-called *Neapolitan Sixth*, the first inversion of the major triad on the flattened super-tonic—thus in C major of Db:

Ex. 77

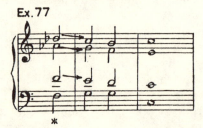

Equipped with three layers of forcefully descending semitones bearing it down into the tonic chord—the Db to C, the Ab to G, the F to E—the chord positively swoops into the key. Ever since the seventeenth century this magnificently dynamic chromatic chord has been part of the stock vocabulary of both a major and a minor key.[1]

*   *   *   *

It remains to say something of the part which chromatic triads play in a minor key. Now or never in fact is the time to tie up the loose end which I left at the conclusion of my chapter on that key, to redeem my promise to explain later how the concords of the 'melodic' minor are handled.

We saw that C's melodic minor scale contained two notes,

---

[1] One other chromatic triad deserves mention: the minor triad on the sub-dominant of a major key—e.g. on F in the key of C major. In the major key its 'minor' quality has a characteristic dark richness. Resolving as it does effortlessly on the tonic and dominant triads it is very frequently employed.

A♮ and B♭, which had no place in the cadences of the harmonic minor imparting the quality of key. This raised the question: how then were handled the triads in which these notes *did* have a place, i.e. in the case of the A♮, the minor triad of D and the major one of F, and in that of the B♭, the minor triad of G and the major ones of E♭ and B♭?

Regarding the A♮ group I will content myself here with the bare statement that one of them, the minor triad of D, is used frequently. The B♭ group, on the other hand, requires a paragraph to itself since, apart from the fact that all three chords are used frequently, two of them, the E♭ and B♭ triads, exercise an important influence on the whole character of a minor key.

Two preliminary observations need to be made here:

(1) the E♭ triad is the tonic chord of C minor's relative major key of E♭, which has every note in common with its descending version;

(2) the B♭ triad is the dominant chord of this relative major key.

Bearing this in mind let us now suppose that in the course of a piece in C minor the dominant seventh of E♭ is sounded, followed by the E♭ tonic chord; if so then willy nilly the key of E♭ major is established. In point of fact this often happens— indeed so often that one can say of a minor key that it has a constitutional tendency to gravitate into the key of its relative major. Thus 'O the Oak and the Ash', after its first two lines in C minor:

Ex. 78

passes imperceptibly into E♭ major:

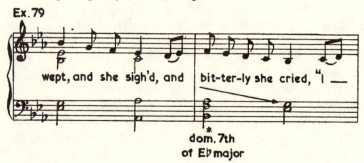

and then imperceptibly back into the home key:

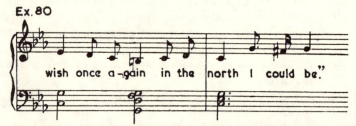

The change is imperceptible because the two chords which bring it about are after all themselves members of the home key. It is this effortless gravitation into the sphere of a contrasting major key which gives to the E♭ and the B♭ triad (converted into a dominant seventh) the importance I spoke of. They confer upon the key, as it were, 'the freedom of the city' of its relative major; thanks to them a minor key has an inherent elasticity, an inherent possibility of major-minor key contrast. As witness 'O the Oak and the Ash'. One of the features of this tune's beauty is the major harmony of 'O she wept and she sigh'd, and bitterly she cried'. Unawares we have been transported to another plane, where momentarily the sky is brighter —but with a brightness which only serves to throw into relief the darkness of the surrounding minor key.

SUMMARY OF CHAPTER XI

The chromatic chords to be studied in this chapter, unlike the dominant sevenths studied above, disrupt the home key without effecting a change into a new one.

The key system, in order to be an instrument of many-sided expression, needed the abnormal disrupting effect of such chromatic chords.

Upon chromatic triads and discords the system imposed the same terms of admission as those imposed upon diatonic discords (see Chapter VIII). As a diatonic dissonance must function melodically as a passing note or in a passing chord, suspension or appoggiatura, so must a chromatic one. Since every note of the diatonic scale is bordered by a chromatic note capable of pulling to it this condition of entry could be easily met.

The following three chromatic triads of a major key are frequently exploited:

(1) The major triad on D, the super-tonic.

Since the triad is built on the 'dominant of the dominant' it sounds at home in the key of C.

(2) The major triad on A♭, the flattened sub-mediant.

The chord sounds foreign, but it has a sensuous charm and melts effortlessly into the resolving tonic chord, the root of which is situated a major third above A♭. Evidently the sensuous charm of this interval is reflected in the relationship of the two chords.

(3) The first inversion of the major triad on D♭, the flattened super-tonic, called the Neapolitan sixth.

The chord sounds foreign but it thrusts dynamically to the tonic triad with which it forms three layers of downward pulling semitone intervals.

The chromatic triads of a minor key

A minor key, with its different ascending and descending 'melodic' versions, contains five triads which play no part in the key-defining cadences of the harmonic minor. These divide into two groups:

(1) The minor triad on D and the major triad on F, containing an A♮.

The minor triad on D is frequently used.

(2) The major triads on E♭ and B♭ and the minor triad on G, containing a B♭.

All three are frequently used and furthermore the E♭ and B♭ triads are respectively the tonic and dominant chords of the 'relative major', E♭ major. The two are so often employed to define this key that it can be said of a minor key that it has an inherent tendency to exploit the effect of major-minor key contrast.

CHAPTER XII

Key Change in the Idiom of the Vienna Classics (I)

IT was not until the age of Haydn (1732–1809), Mozart (1756–91) and Beethoven (1770–1827) that the resource of the remote key change came to be fully exploited and its great potentialities realized.

My first step must be to show why the idiom of these masters lent itself to the development of the resource, and why that of Bach and Handel did not.

I remarked above that harmonies are perceived both vertically and horizontally and that the relative vividness of the two planes depends upon the style of a work—that an unaccompanied motet for two voices is experienced more horizontally, a harmonized tune such as the National Anthem more vertically. Bach's and Handel's was primarily a horizontal idiom. For them harmony's main function was to provide the requisite conventionally well-built framework for the edifice of their counterpoint. Thus generally it is only in music admitting of looseness of structure and calling for effects of surprise—in recitatives, ariosos, and fantasias—that they let themselves go (Bach especially) and venture into remote keys. A striking example of this primarily functional view of harmony can be seen in their attitude to the so-called *figured bass*. All the ensemble music of the period included a bass part for a keyboard instrument, written as a single line, below which were set figures indicating the chords to be played. In supplying these chords the player was expected to improvise individual counterpoints at his discretion; to go beyond this and introduce novel harmonic effects for their own sake would have been a betrayal of his office. From the point of view of Bach and Handel and their period harmony was primarily a means to an end; and this being so it is understandable that theirs was not an idiom favourable to the cultivation of the resource of the remote key change.

In the case of these two masters the limits which their idiom imposed were, of course, a supreme source of strength. That blazing power and splendour of Handel's great choruses lies, as we saw, in the sheer simplicity of his harmony. This simplicity shines through his counterpoint and this notwithstanding the fact (is this perhaps the inmost essence of Handel's genius?) that it is a counterpoint containing a complex wealth of melodic-rhythmic contrast between the strands which compose it (think of the thrilling rush of the sopranos' semiquavers above the tenors' 'unto us a Son is given' in *Messiah*). Bach's counterpoint is very different. His themes and counter-themes tend to be florid, decked with inessential notes; their interlacing produces above the simple harmonic basis a complex super-structure of passing and appoggiatura chords, often dissonant and chromatic, even recondite, anticipating (as we shall have occasion to observe later) the complexities of nineteenth- and of twentieth-century harmony, conveying a painful depth and intensity of feeling unknown to Handel.

*　　*　　*　　*

It is a truism that the path of history is a spiral of twisting, conflicting forces; that a struggle transforms both parties for good or evil; that whatever the outcome a previous situation never repeats itself. The dynasty of the Stuarts was restored in 1660, but the Restoration was no mere *status quo ante bellum*: profiting from the tragic example of his predecessor, Charles II died in bed.

The path of music's history is also a spiral. In the early seventeenth century a reaction takes place against the complex polyphony of the Church in favour of a simpler homophonic idiom. In the course of the century the success of the reaction leads to the building of a key system. Later in the century the path once again curves back to polyphony—but of a different kind, based on the key system, culminating in the next century in the masterpieces of Bach and Handel. But by that time another reaction is under way: Bach is regarded as bombastic, confused, and out of date; once again the spiral is curving back to simple homophony.

It would be outside the scope of this book to trace stage by stage the subsequent dazzling flight of the spiral during and after the eighteenth century. Here it is only necessary to realize that polyphony enjoyed a second Golden Age in Bach and Handel because polyphony satisfied men's instinct for artistic elaboration, as a jejune homophonic idiom, confined only to the most obvious key relationships, could never do; and that it satisfied it so completely as to rule out for the time being the need for any other resource. When in due course this need arose it was met by the cultivation of the remote key change, a resource leading to an expansion of the key system on the grandest possible scale.

*   *   *   *

Understanding of this grand expansion of the key system can only be obtained by closely studying a particular example of a work by one of the Vienna Classics. But we are not yet ready to undertake such a study. To equip ourselves, we must in the first place outline the basic features of the most typical and important form of the period: sonata-form. And in the second place we must enlarge our knowledge of modulation, a topic which hitherto we have discussed only in the restricted context of a piece modulating to related keys. When these matters have been dealt with we shall be able to address ourselves to the music itself.

SUMMARY OF CHAPTER XII

The purpose of this chapter is to explain in general terms why the idiom of Bach and Handel did not, and why that of the Vienna Classics did, lend itself to the cultivation of the resource of the remote key change.

Bach and Handel's attitude to harmony was primarily functional: it served the purpose of providing a conventionally well-built framework for the edifice of their counterpoint.

In the early eighteenth century a reaction was under way in favour of a simpler, more homophonic idiom. In the course of the century the instinct for artistic elaboration, hitherto fulfilled in counterpoint, found a fresh outlet in cultivation of the remote key change, leading to an expansion of the key system on the grandest possible scale.

In order to understand the nature of this expansion through analysis of an actual work two preliminary steps are necessary:

(1) the basic features of sonata-form must be outlined;
(2) the topic of modulation must be further studied.

CHAPTER XIII

Key Change in the Idiom of the Vienna Classics (II)

SONATA-FORM is a topic so often dealt with in popular books on music, that I shall assume here that the reader is familiar at any rate with its basic features and that it is not incumbent upon me to do more than refresh his memory. Thus he will have read that a movement in sonata-form falls into three parts as follows:

(1) the *Exposition* containing
   the *First Subject* in the key of the tonic;
   the *Bridge Passage* modulating to a related key;
   the *Second Subject* in the related key;

(2) the *Development Section* containing
   key changes to new keys, related and/or remote, and consisting of elaboration of material of the exposition and/or of *episodes* in which new material is introduced;

(3) the *Recapitulation* containing
   the *First Subject* in the key of the tonic;
   the Bridge Passage, this time modulating back to the key of the tonic;
   the Second Subject in the key of the tonic.

A movement in sonata-form may or may not also contain an *Introduction*, and be rounded off by a concluding *Coda*.

This design has certain familiar implications, of which I will briefly remind the reader as follows:

(1) It was a design worked out empirically in the eighteenth century and only subsequently by nineteenth-century theorists stereotyped and given its title of sonata-form. Thus actual examples only conform to the nineteenth-century blue-print in a general sense; over and over again in details, sometimes important ones, they depart from it.

(2) The term 'subject' does not connote a theme (as it does in the case of a fugue), but a section cast in a single key. Very often a first subject has a melodic unity giving it the character of a 'subject' in the fugal sense; thus here the two meanings of the term are liable to overlap and cause confusion. Not so in the case of the second subject which usually contains more than one theme and of which the unifying factor is solely that it is cast in a single key.

(3) If the movement is in a major key, the related key of the second subject is normally that of the dominant; if in the minor key, that of the relative major.

(4) The basic structural feature of the development section is neither its thematic elaboration nor its episodes, but its continuous shifting of tonality through keys other than those of the first and second subject. The greater the scale of the movement, the greater the range of this shifting and the more thoroughgoing the exploitation of the remote keys.

Regarding the design as a whole it remains to point out here that, divided as it is into three sections, its pattern is fundamentally ternary,[1] and further that it is a pattern according the widest possible scope to the departing-in-order-to-return logic of tonality. In the short tune of 'O God our Help', with its point of maximum distance a mere cadential modulation to the key of the dominant, we saw that logic in embryo. In the longer tune of 'Where the Bee sucks', with its whole middle section cast in the key of the dominant, we saw it expanded through the ternary principle. Now we are seeing this principle raised to its highest potency. The pattern of 'Where the Bee sucks' with its two alternating keys could be diagrammatically rendered by the following simple arrangement of straight lines to represent passages cast in a single key and diagonal arrows to represent modulations:

The pattern of a movement in sonata-form would need to be represented by some such complicated diagram as follows:

---

[1] The textbook description of sonata-form as a 'compound binary' pattern reflects its historical evolution, a matter not dealt with in these pages.

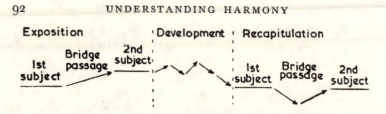

Rough and ready though it is, this diagram at least has the merit of showing that the key changes of the development section form the intermediate link of a ternary structure—in fact that they are the basic structural feature not only of the development section itself, but of the whole form.

*   *   *   *

We must now take our bearings in regard to the part which modulation plays upon this wide stage of sonata-form.

It will be convenient here to employ an image. To each key, we know, is attached a set of five related keys. Let us think of these five keys as satellite keys and of the key around which they cluster as the central body of a sort of planetary tonal system. Thus around the planet of C major cluster its satellites, G and F major, D, E, and A minor:[1]

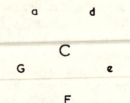

In the light of this image let us now briefly glance back at our previous examples of key change. In the short piece in binary form of the type of 'O God our Help' or 'Early one morning', containing brief passing and cadential changes, to all intents and purposes we never leave the central body: the function of such changes, as I said, is not really to change key at all, but rather to expand the range of the original key (see page 76). In the somewhat longer piece in ternary form of the type of 'Where the Bee sucks' we leave the central body, go

[1] Major keys in this and following diagrams are denoted by capital letters.

from C major to G major and definitely stay there. But throughout our stay, I pointed out, the relation of the new key to the
old one is vivid in our minds. We never cease to feel that this
new key we are in is the key of C's dominant—in other words
that it is a satellite of C's.

Suppose, however, that a composer in passing from C to
G major is not content that the stay in G should be experienced
merely as a visit to one of C's satellites; suppose he wishes us
for the time being to lose sight altogether of the old key, to feel
that we are not at the periphery of C's tonal system, *but at the
centre of G's*. One method of causing us to feel this is to build up
a progression which instead of proceeding, as in 'Where the
Bee sucks', direct from C to G, thus:

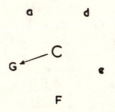

takes a devious route. It proceeds first to D major, *which falls
within G's tonal system, but not in C's*, and then from D major
passes on into G major:

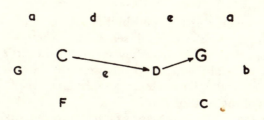

The effect of the temporary visit to D is to destroy G's character
as C's satellite and set it up as the centre of its own tonal system.
Thus Mozart in the bridge passage of the first movement of
Eine Kleine Nachtmusik (which for the purpose of this discussion
I shall transpose into the key of C major) establishes as a tonal
centre the key, G major, of his second subject by a brief
detour into D major:

Ex.81

dom. 7th
of D major

Bars 25-7

In this brief detour of Mozart's we are catching a first glimpse of the part, new to us, which we are going to see modulation playing upon the stage of sonata-form. Modulation, when we originally met it in 'O God our Help', was simply a method of getting 'without pain' from key to key by the interposing of a chord which cushioned the impact of the new key's dominant chord. In 'Where the Bee sucks' we saw modulation employed on a larger scale, saw it taking the form of a four-bar passage containing passing and cadential changes into the new key of the middle section, giving advance notice of the new key and acting as a sort of bridge into it. Now we are seeing modulation taking on yet another role: no longer is it merely a method of 'avoiding pain' or of 'giving advance notice' but of *building up a new key by interposing between it and the old one a temporary change to another key.*

What immense artistic possibilities this form of modulating key change holds we shall see below when we come to discuss in detail the first movement of Mozart's 'Jupiter' Symphony. Before we can do this we must, however roughly and schematically, form a more complete picture of the various workings of the method itself.

In our *Eine Kleine Nachtmusik* example only one key, D major, is interposed between the keys of the first and second subjects. A modulation can take a much more extended course than this brief detour.

In what follows I will indicate in bare outline some of the possibilities open to a composer.

(1) A modulation could pass through A minor and E minor to D major and thence to G:

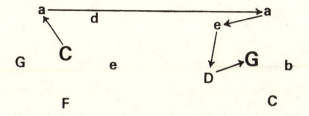

A minor and E minor are satellites which the tonal systems of C and G major share. In passing through these keys before reaching G major the modulation is therefore creating an effect of tonal ambiguity: not until we reach D major can we realize that the threshold has been crossed out of one tonal system into another.

(2) A modulation could pass through A minor, E minor *and B minor* to D major and thence to G:

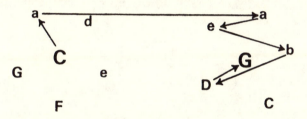

B minor, like D major, is a satellite of G's, not C's. The visit to it accordingly has the effect of strengthening the build-up of G's tonal system. The conjunction, A minor–E minor–B minor–D major *suggests* the central key, to which each acts as satellite, in the sense that to hear these four keys in succession is to feel *already* that we are in G's system and to anticipate the eventual close into that key.

(3) After entering G's system the modulation could double on its tracks and re-enter C's—and then finally return into G's. Thus it might in the first place go to E minor and B minor in G's system:

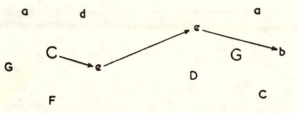

then change its mind, go back to E minor and follow it by F major with which E minor lies together in C's—not G's—system:

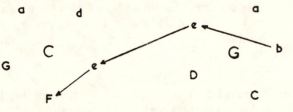

and then finally turn G major-wards, going this time via A minor:

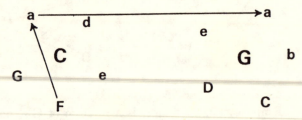

The effect of this roaming around among keys not belonging together in any one tonal system is again to create a feeling of ambiguity: it is as though one were wandering at large in a sort of tonal no-man's-land. For this reason it is obviously a very powerful resource, since the greater the tension generated during the course of an extended modulation the greater the effect of the eventual establishing of the new key.

These various forms of extended modulation are capable of an even greater elaboration when the new key is not, as in all the cases we have so far considered, a related, but a remote one.

When the new key is a remote one, the question no longer arises of having to destroy its previous character as satellite in the old key's system: being remote, it lies outside the old system. The composer has only to go there and he will create an effect of surprise. He can cushion this effect by interpolating a 'pain'-removing modulating chord or two: or he can abolish it altogether by employing an extended modulation. He will make preliminary visits to the new key's satellite keys and by so doing gradually acclimatize the ear to the strange atmosphere of the remote region *by going in the first place to satellite keys which the old system shares with the new one.*

Suppose, for example, the passage is from C major to D major. The ear will be acclimatized if before we visit a satellite of D's which it does not share with C—i.e. A major, or B minor or F♯ minor—we visit a satellite which C and D have in common—i.e. G major or E minor:

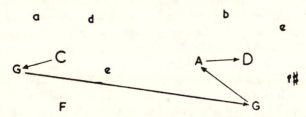

Suppose, however, two keys share no satellite. Then the ear can be acclimatized by making the modulation pass through one of the home key's satellites whose tonal system *does* share a key with that of the new key's. Thus a modulation from C major to A major could start by going to E minor and thence to E minor's satellite B minor, which is also A major's:

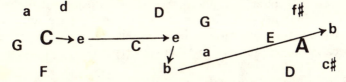

When two keys are so remote from each other that not even the systems of their satellites possess a key in common, then the process of acclimatization could be still more drawn out. The modulation could proceed through a whole series of keys in order to find a point of contact. Suppose, for example, we were modulating from C major to F♯ major: by the route outlined we could get as far as A major: from thence we could proceed to C♯ minor in A's system; then to B major in C♯ minor's; and so through B major at last to F♯ major's:

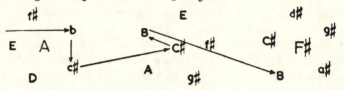

It can be imagined what a wealth and variety of tonal ambiguity can be created in the course of such elaborate far-flung modulations to the remoter keys. Take the comparatively simple example of the above modulation from C major to A major via the intermediary E minor–B minor connexion. Instead of going straight on to A major the modulation could veer off its course and make a tour of E minor's system, building up the expectation that this key is to be its goal—then at the last minute surprise the ear by swerving off into A major after all. Or instead it might double on its tracks and swerve back momentarily into C major's system—and then proceed to A major by another route. If instead of A major the goal were the much remoter key of F♯ major, the modulation could —— but let the reader who is so minded work out the possibilities for himself!

*   *   *   *

After this discussion of the mechanics of modulation we are now in a position to consider the part which key changes play in one of the most splendid of all the many splendid examples of a classical movement in sonata-form, the first movement of Mozart's 'Jupiter' Symphony. So doing, let us also at the same time—since neither this nor any other single movement illustrates all the possibilities—hold ourselves free, whenever the occasion arises, to refer to other masterpieces.

The First Subject

I remarked above that the subject of a movement in sonata-form is cast in a single key; it would have been more illuminating to have said: cast in the *tonal system* of a single key. Thus Mozart here, after commencing in C major:

Ex.82

hints at G major:

and then modulates back into C major:

After this diversion he brings the subject to a close with a series of forcible cadences in C major, driving home that this is to be the central key of the symphony.

The Bridge Passage

The bridge passage of *Eine Kleine Nachtmusik* is a comparatively slight affair, touching only one intermediary key and thematically insignificant. This one lasts for thirty-two bars, touches more than one intermediary key, and carries the thematic argument of the first subject a decisive stage further. Example 82 itself introduces it, but this time set below a graceful counterpoint:

Ex. 85

Bars 24-7

When we come to discuss the development section we shall see what a vital part in the argument of the movement as a whole the above bridge passage version of Example 82 plays. Indeed in a context such as this—and it is no exception—the very term bridge passage is something of a misnomer: what concerns Mozart here is not only the immediate task of bridging the tonal gap between first and second subject: in the act of bridging it, in the act of modulating, he is laying the foundations of the movement as a whole.

The Second Subject

Since a second subject, unlike a first, normally contains several melodic ideas it needs a correspondingly greater freedom of modulation in order to deploy them. Thus it is likely to go outside the tonal system of its key. Mozart does so here. After commencing the subject with a long passage strictly in the key of G major he swings himself on to the dominant seventh of what the context leads one to expect will prove to be that of G's sub-dominant, C major:

Ex. 86

Bars 78-80

The above full bar's rest is broken by the whole orchestra thundering out fortissimo the tonic chord of C *minor*. For a moment we are in another world—then the E♭ of the C minor chord sharpens and very soon we are back in G major again. We hear a new theme, unpretentious, innocently graceful, yet destined to play a great part later in the movement:

Ex. 87

Bars 101-2

Bars 107-8

The Development Section

I will consider this section first from the point of view of its tonal structure. Later I will discuss its thematic structure and endeavour to show how the two are inter-related.

The section begins with a sudden modulation to E♭ major. After the long sojourn of the second subject in G major the sudden modulation comes as a delightful relief, the more so since this particular remote key to which it transports us is that of G major's exotically delightful flattened sub-mediant chord (whose qualities we discussed above in the chapter on the chromatic triads).

Mozart then proceeds to make us feel at home in the new key. For twelve bars we remain strictly in E♭ major; then we are taken off on a tour of some of E♭'s satellite keys; then we return to E♭ itself, feeling more than ever at home there. Once more we leave the key, this time for good: indeed from now on the whole of the development section can be regarded as one vast modulation heading for the—from the point of view of

E♭ major—remote key of the first subject, C major. From E♭ major Mozart goes to its satellite G minor, and thence to G minor's satellite D minor, which is also C major's:

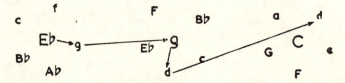

From D minor Mozart moves over to A minor and lingers there a few bars. F major follows. It looks as though we are passing definitely into C major's tonal system and that the section is about to end:

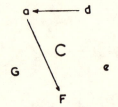

But no: having reached F major the modulation proceeds to veer out of C major's system and double on its tracks; it goes to F major's satellite, G minor, which is also E♭ major's:

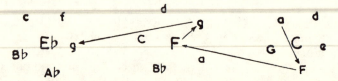

From G minor Mozart then moves across again to A minor; this time he shakes off for good the E♭ association and stays in C major's system building up the re-entry of the first subject which will bring the development section to an end and launch the recapitulation.

Now let us consider the section from the point of view of its thematic structure. It begins, we saw, with a sudden modulation to the romantically delightful key of E♭ major; Mozart, relying on the sheer charm of the key to give a fresh lease of life to familiar material, transposes into it the second subject theme of Example 87.

Ex. 88

Bars 123-4

Throughout the ensuing tour of E♭ major's satellites, the return to that key and the modulation to G minor and D minor Mozart is putting the second subject theme through a strenuous course of canonic development:

Ex. 89

Bars 133-5

From D minor, as we saw, Mozart then moves over to A minor and F major, conveying the impression, which in the event proves false, that he is passing definitively into C major's system and ending the section. He cunningly reinforces this false impression by at this point sounding the first subject, indelibly associated in our minds with the home key. This time we hear it in F major; not quite in its original form, but linked to the graceful counterpoint with which it opened the bridge passage:

Ex. 90

Bars 161-4

8

Saturated as we have been by the sustained E♭ major development of the second subject, this sudden F major reminder of the
opening theme of the movement has an indescribable force: it
is as though, having travelled far afield, we were beholding a
distant view of home. Indescribable, too, is the effect of the
next bars in which the modulation doubles on its tracks and
veers E♭-major-wards through G minor. Mozart does nothing
here but repeat the first subject and its bridge passage counterpoint: as we hear the familiar themes slipping further away
from the orbit of the home key, it is as though the distant
view were a mirage, receding as we approach:

Bars 165-8

But Mozart soon makes amends, soon drives finally into
C major's system. As he does so he develops the semiquaver
triplet of the first subject, brandishes it forth in a series of
lightning thrusts, triumphantly fights his way home with it:

Bars 171-2

When at length Mozart arrives home it is to re-state the first
subject in its original form, shorn of the graceful counterpoint

with which it had been linked in that F major version and the following bars. Thus our pleasure in hearing it again is a double one: the theme is in the right key at last, and in the right form. Tonal and thematic logic correspond.

The Recapitulation

Mozart's recapitulation is exact—except, of course, at the bridge passage where the sonata-form structure obliges him to frame a modulation which instead of leading to the key of the dominant for the second subject will lead back to the key of the tonic, in other words a modulation which will double on its tracks and return to its point of departure. In order that the second subject, cast now in the key of the tonic, should have the freshness of impact which it originally had in the key of the dominant, Mozart brings about a thorough clearing of the air of C major by sweeping out into the remote keys of E♭ major and F minor. This he does without altering or extending his thematic material. In the great G minor symphony, on the other hand, he seizes the occasion to build up a development which is one of the high spots of the whole first movement.

*   *   *   *

The picture I have been attempting to draw of the part played by key change in the idiom of the Vienna Classics will not be complete without some mention of the two features of sonata-form missing from the first movement of the 'Jupiter', the Introduction and the Coda.

Besides being a striking piece of music in its own right, capable of arresting and holding attention, an introduction must serve the purpose of acting as a foil to what is to follow. From the tonal point of view two main ways in which the classical introduction achieves this purpose can be distinguished. One way is at the outset to create the expectation that a certain key is destined to be the tonic of the movement and then to postpone the confirming of this expectation until the actual entry of the first subject. This is the way of Mozart in the great E♭ Symphony, No. 39. He starts by establishing the key of E♭ major, but only briefly, and then proceeds to move grandly through a number of E♭'s satellite keys: as these keys succeed each other, building up E♭'s tonal system, the expectation persists of an eventual return to and dwelling in that key. Thus when at length, with a sudden quickening of tempo, the E♭ first subject enters, not only are we charmed by the theme itself, but gratified that at last this expectation is rewarded. Thanks to the introduction the entry of the theme, for all its air of unselfconscious innocence, is a momentous event.

Another more drastic way of enhancing the impact of a first subject is illustrated by the introduction to Beethoven's Fourth Symphony. Beethoven does nothing to create the expectation that B♭ major is to be the key of the first movement: on the contrary, he starts by establishing B♭ *minor* and from thence modulates to the very remote sphere of B major; only in the latter half of the introduction does he begin to steer B♭-major-wards, and only when the first subject itself comes rushing in does he finally plump for that key. Hence the dazzling effect of that entry: starting from the depths of a minor key and pursuing a wandering road therefrom we suddenly emerge into the glorious sunlight of the corresponding major key. The gloomy start was a false one.

Beethoven's handling of the coda is equally distinctive. Mozart's and Haydn's codas normally have the character of an afterthought rounding off the recapitulation: built on a slight scale, keeping within the tonal system of the home key, they do not modify the essential ABA structure of the movement as a whole. Not so some of Beethoven's codas: in the great 'odd-number' symphonies—the Third, the Fifth, the Seventh, the Ninth—the coda, far from being a mere afterthought rounding off the recapitulation, is a mighty bonfire, triumphantly cele-brating the close of the movement. In the finale of the Fifth the celebration is conducted within the tonal system of the home key: the impact of the themes, the impetus of the rhythm and the tremendous dynamics of the passage carry the music to a supreme pitch of intensity and excitement. Usually, however, Beethoven demands a greater tonal elbow-room: thus in the coda of the first movement of the 'Eroica', having brought the recapitulation to its resounding conclusion in E♭ major he shatters E♭'s system by a sudden hurling into it of the triad of the remote key of D♭ major:

Ex. 93

Bars 557-9

As though this were not enough, Beethoven then, instead of going on to establish the key of Db (which that tremendous triad had led us to expect) startles us by hurling forth yet another remote triad, that of C major:

Ex. 94

Bars 560-2

C major he does establish. From this point outside the orbit of the home key Beethoven then drives back into it for the last time, building up the final heroic celebration which brings the movement to its close.

SUMMARY OF CHAPTER XIII

(1) *Sonata-form*

A movement in sonata-form falls into three parts:

(i) *The Exposition* containing a first subject in the key of the tonic, a bridge passage modulating to a related key, and a second subject in the related key.

(ii) *The Development Section* containing key changes to new keys, related and/or remote, and elaboration of the exposition and/or episodes.

(iii) *The Recapitulation* containing the first subject in the key of the tonic, the bridge passage modulating to the key of the tonic and the second subject in the key of the tonic.

A movement may be preceded by an introduction and rounded off by a coda.

The tri-partite structure can be regarded as an expansion of the ternary pattern of *Where the Bee sucks*, whose first and third sections were cast in the key of the tonic, and its middle section in that of the dominant. Here the middle section ranges through a number of remote keys. The depart-in-order-to-return logic of tonality can find its maximum scope.

(2) *Modulation*

In order to understand the role of modulation in sonata-form it is necessary to review the nature of the relationship existing between a key and a related key.

A key's related keys bear to it the relationship of a group of satellites clustered around a central body. A key can be regarded as the focal point of a tonal system, formed by its five satellite related keys.

Modulation in sonata-form, besides serving the purposes described above (see Chapter IX), performs the function of destroying a related key's quality as satellite and setting it up as the focal point of its own tonal system.

This is achieved if the modulation, instead of proceeding directly from the home key to its related satellite key, pays a preliminary visit to one of the latter's satellite keys, e.g. if instead of proceeding directly from C major to G major it goes via G major's satellite D major.

This method of indirect modulation is an instrument capable of being applied in different ways:

(1) By proceeding to the new key via a satellite which it shares with the original one it can create an effect of tonal ambiguity.

(2) By proceeding via more than one of the new key's satellites it can protract and strengthen the build-up of its tonal system.

(3) It can 'double on its tracks', i.e. after a preliminary visit to one or more of the related key's satellites it can return to a satellite belonging to the original tonal system, and then finally proceed into the system of the new key. The tonal ambiguity created by such an extended modulation powerfully enhances the effect of the eventual establishing of the new key.

When a new key is remote the method of indirect modulation is capable of being applied in a similar way and if need be on a more elaborate scale.

(1) In order to cushion the shock produced by a sudden passage to a remote key, the modulation can proceed via a satellite which the new key and the old share in common.

(2) If two keys share no satellite in common the modulation can be protracted by making it proceed via a satellite of the home key, whose system *does* share a satellite with that of the remote key. Thus a modulation from C major to the remote key of A major could go via E minor and B minor. E minor is a satellite of C's and B minor a satellite of E minor which it shares with A major.

(3) If two keys are so remote that not even the systems of their satellites possess a key in common, the modulation can be drawn out through a whole series of keys in order to find a point of contact. Thus a modulation from C major to F♯ major, having reached A major's system via E minor and B minor could proceed to F♯ major via C♯ minor in A major's system, thence to B major in C♯ minor's system, and so through B major at last into F♯ major's system.

(4) The modulation can 'double on its tracks'.

In the Development Section of the first movement of the 'Jupiter' Symphony Mozart employs such a modulation. The starting point of the modulation is E♭ major and its goal C major. Mozart starts by going through G minor to D minor, which falls within C major's system. He then proceeds to build up C major's system by visiting two other of its satellites, A minor and F major. From F major he then turns back to G minor, which is E♭ major's satellite. From thence he moves to A minor and thereafter remains in C major's system, strenuously building it up in preparation for the re-entry of the first subject which will launch the recapitulation.

CHAPTER XIV

Chromaticism and the Dominant Seventh[1] (1)

BROACHING the topic of chromaticism, I observed that the key system, to be an artistic medium capable of expressing the gamut of human feeling, stood in need of the incalculable, abnormal, disrupting element of chromaticism. I promised the reader that in the idiom of the Vienna Classics he would see that the system acquired a fresh and immensely widened scope through the resource of modulation to the remote keys of chromatic triads; and further that in the romantic idiom of the nineteenth century he would see chromaticism modify and transform the very system itself. In these penultimate chapters of this book it remains to fulfil this second promise.

Before the promise can be fulfilled we must retrace our steps and—for the last time—re-enter the laboratory of the earlier chapters in order once more to put under the microscope the dominant seventh, that key-establishing chord which—as we have now had abundant opportunity to observe—is the harmonic pivot of the whole system. We must study it from two points of view, at first sight quite different from each other, but, as we shall see, in reality intimately and importantly connected.

The reader will recall that when first we encountered the dominant seventh we started by examining it from the point of view of its structure. We found that the build of the chord corresponded very closely with that of the Harmonic Series and assumed a connexion between this and the fact that for all its dissonance the chord is nevertheless harmonious— 'indeed so much so that we can postpone its resolution in order to enjoy the luxury of dwelling upon it for its own sweet sake'. Regarding the harmoniousness of the dominant seventh there

[1] To facilitate the reading of chords, many of the examples in this and the following chapter will be rendered in transposed keys.

is this further observation to make: it confers upon the chord and its respective inversions the power, which hitherto we have only seen exercised by the triad, of *acting as the resolving chord of an appoggiatura*—doing this even though it itself, being a discord, will ultimately have to resolve. To put it metaphorically: although a sinner itself in need of absolution, a dominant seventh is pure enough to confer the grace of absolution upon others. Both in a major and in a minor key it confers this grace upon three appoggiatura chords:

Ex.95   MAJOR KEY   MINOR KEY

dominant   dominant dominant dominant dominant dominant
major   eleventh   major   minor   eleventh   minor
ninth   thirteenth ninth   thirteenth

The chords are named according to the interval formed between their root and their respective appoggiatura notes. Thus in the major key we have the dominant major ninth, dominant eleventh, and dominant major thirteenth; and in a minor key the dominant minor ninth, dominant eleventh, and dominant minor thirteenth.

Although all these 'dominant discords', as they are collectively called, were used freely—inverted, as well as in root position—throughout the eighteenth and nineteenth centuries it behoves us here to concentrate attention upon the dominant major and minor ninths, since it is these two which illustrate most forcibly the transformation which the key system underwent in the romantic idiom.

Consider first the sheer sound of the dominant major ninth. Since, like the dominant seventh, it is a 'natural' discord—a slightly flattened A comes next after the slightly flattened F in the ladder of the fundamental G's overtones—it is harmonious. And yet it has a very characteristic tang of its own. The dominant seventh is sweet and comparatively serene; it wants to be resolved, but not urgently. The ninth is bitter-sweet and anything but serene. With a sort of enjoyable, luxurious anguish it yearns to be resolved. It is indeed the chord of chords for the expression of romantic yearning, the chord beloved of Wagner, Liszt, Tchaikovsky, Puccini, the chord in the twentieth century shunned by every self-respecting anti-romantic composer like the plague.

Since it is a chord of five notes and part-writing is normally four-voiced the ninth is more often than not rendered in a reduced version, minus one of its notes. This impairs its character—but only very slightly if, as is frequently the case, the omitted note is the root of the chord:

Ex. 96

Evidently what gives the ninth its peculiar bitter-sweet tang is the combination of the appoggiatura note, A, with the three *upper* notes of the dominant seventh, with F, D, and B rather than with G, the root itself. The parent root engenders the combination, but does not stamp its character—it is, as it were, the children here who do the talking.

Let us now observe the dominant major ninth in action. It appears in this lilting phrase from Susanna's 'Deh vieni' in *The Marriage of Figaro*:

Ex. 97

Here the potential romanticism of the chord is held in check by the gracious lilt of the *Siciliano* rhythm, which binds the structure of the aria and stamps its character. Even though the appoggiatura-note forms the climax of the phrase, its pathos is contained—and this is true broadly of all dominant discords as they were used in the eighteenth century. Their expressiveness was kept in bounds by the unfolding rhythmic pattern of a piece as a whole.

Compare now this phrase with the culminating phrase of the great theme of the variations of the final movement of Beethoven's late Piano Sonata, Op. 109, in which once again we see a dominant major ninth:[1]

Ex. 98

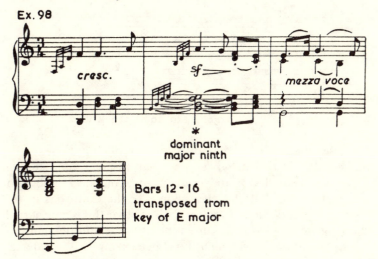

dominant
major ninth

Bars 12 - 16
transposed from
key of E major

Here the expressiveness of the chord has a much greater scope. Occurring once again at a climax, this time it is marked *sforzando*; a crescendo sweeps up to it; an arpeggio spreads it out; it is held for the length of a dotted crotchet. Whereas it would be a capital crime (albeit a frequently committed one) to slacken the lilt of Susanna's aria, here, if the beauty of the music is to make its full effect, the pianist positively must linger, be it ever so slightly, on the chord and steep us in its bittersweet romanticism.

This example of the late Beethoven typifies the handling of the chord throughout the nineteenth century. But it also underwent a further development, namely that, being like its parent dominant seventh a harmonious 'natural' discord, it too began to breed appoggiaturas. As the dominant seventh begat the major ninth and its brother dominant discords, so in its turn the major ninth (and here one recalls that remark quoted above that 'the history of music is written in the appoggiatura) begat the 'appoggiatura'd' major ninth. Thus

[1] Beethoven here uses the chord in its first inversion.

Tchaikovsky in that famous second subject of the first movement of the 'Pathétique' does more than merely linger on the
chord's bitter-sweetness:

Ex. 99

Bars 99-101
transposed from
key of D major

dominant
major ninth combined with appoggiatura
note C♯

He gives the knife another turn by introducing, beneath the
pathetic fall of the melody's appoggiatura-note, another such
note, an accented C♯, and resolving it upon the D above for
which it yearns. The bitter-sweetness of the ninth has in this
'appoggiatura'd' form—and we shall see that this is true of such
chords generally—become intensified to an exquisite agony.

The romantic trend which the above examples illustrate can
be summed up quite simply. The practice of 'appoggiaturing'
(if I may be allowed the verb) the dominant seventh and then
going one step further and appoggiaturing the appoggiatura
meant that the fundamental harmony of a dominant seventh
was being sustained in order to support a superstructure
growing ever more intensely expressive. In the idiom of the
great sonata-form movements of the Vienna Classics, informed
by a logic of harmonic *motion*, dominant sevenths fulfilled
another purpose. To make its effect that logic not only could
dispense with highly charged moments of appoggiatura pathos,
but was bound to: key change being the essence of the argument, dominant sevenths and their resolving triads must in all
their naked purity be implied by a movement's themes and
through them permeate the whole work. They permeate the
first movement of the 'Jupiter', which we studied. In the same
way they permeate Beethoven's great movements. Beethoven's
themes indeed are often carved out of mere rhythmically
organized arpeggios, spreading out the fundamental harmony
of a triad—as, to take the most famous instance of all, these
bars of the mighty first movement of the Ninth:

Ex. 100

To have encumbered such a theme with distractingly expressive appoggiaturas would have been to blunt the edge of the tonal argument and to have clogged the rhythmic drive of the movement as a whole.

*   *   *   *

We must now direct our attention to the dominant minor ninth, a chord which, although it has a great deal in common with the major ninth, has a special function throwing light upon the romantic transformation of the key system from another aspect.

First let us see what the chord has in common with the major ninth. To begin with, it too, is used in a four-note version, the omitted note being the root. And up to a point it has a similar character: it too can be described as 'bitter-sweet and anything but serene': it too yearns to be resolved. On the other hand it is a minor chord, with a mournful edge to it, an edge keen enough to penetrate and make itself felt without any deflecting of an established rhythm. Whereas the major ninth, as we saw, did not come into its own until the romantic era, the mournful tragic expressiveness of the minor chord was fully exploited in the eighteenth century—for example in this eloquent bar from the 'Oh, pity me' of the *St Matthew Passion*:

Ex. 101

dominant
minor ninth

Bar 5
transposed from
key of B minor

In the Chromatic Fantasy we also find Bach, in the grief-laden closing passage, forestalling the nineteenth-century practice of 'appoggiaturing' the appoggiatura:

Ex. 102

from Bar 4 from end
transposed from key of
D minor

*
dominant
minor ninth combined with appoggiatura
note E♭

Not that the nineteenth century was incapable of going beyond this. In the following passage from *Parsifal*, in which the 'appoggiatured' appoggiatura is held for the value of a full semibreve and the resolution of the harmony postponed, Wagner draws from the chord an utterance of sheer agony:

Ex. 103

transposed
from key of
A minor

"rootless" dominant
minor ninth combined with appoggiatura
note E♭

So much for the parallel between the major and the minor ninth. Now we must consider that special function of the minor ninth which, I said, throws light upon the romantic transformation of the key system from another aspect.

A clue to this function is provided by a characteristic of the rootless version, which the above examples have not illustrated. If the chord is delivered with the resolution of the appoggiatura note delayed in order that it should make its effect purely and simply as a chord: Ex. 104

it has an uncanny sinister quality, a spine-chilling ambiguity, as though somehow it were poised perilously on the brink of a terrifying abyss. Terrifying indeed is the effect of the chord as Mozart thus delivers it at the tremendous moment of the arrival of the Statue at Don Giovanni's banquet:

Ex. 105

transposed from
key of D minor

Other examples leap to the pen: the child's cry 'Mein Vater, mein Vater' in *Erlkönig*; the tyrant Pisarro's 'Ha! welch'ein Augenblick' in *Fidelio*; the flesh-creeping scene of the Wolfglen in *Der Freischütz*; the plotting of Ortrud and Telramund in *Lohengrin*. Indeed, from Gluck to Wagner in almost any scene of terror or mystery the main brunt of expression is borne by this rootless version of the dominant minor ninth—the so-called chord of the diminished seventh.

This aptness of the diminished seventh for horrific expression has a technical basis. The chord differs from its parent minor ninth in this significant respect, that whereas the five notes of the latter combine diatonically in a single minor key—in our example, the key of C minor—the rootless B, D, F, and A♭ of its diminished seventh version *occur together in three other minor keys, and moreover occur together in the same context, namely, as the rootless version of the dominant minor ninths of these other keys.* Thus the dominant minor ninth of the key of A minor is E–G♯–B–D–F: . Take away the root, E, and convert the G♯ into an A♭ (as thanks to the dispensation of equal temperament you can) and the chord you produce will be the same as the

Ex. 106

diminished seventh in C minor: . Similarly the dominant ninth of E♭ minor is B♭–D–F–A♭–C♭ :

 and of F♯ minor, C♯–E♯–G♯–B–D :

. Remove their roots, and convert the C♭ of

the one into a B, and the E♯ and G♯ of the other into an F and
an A♭, and again you have the same chord:

Ex. 107

Evidently, then, from a purely technical viewpoint the
diminished seventh is a remarkable chord. Nor does the story
end here. There remains to point out this further fact regarding
it and its parent ninth, namely, that although they are chromatic in a major key, their functioning there has the same con-
gruity and forcefulness that it has in a minor one:

Ex. 108

in minor key

in major key

The powerful downward thrust of the chromatic A♭ to the
dominant propels the chords into the major key and makes
them at home there. Like the chromatic triads, which we
studied above, they are in fact part of the stock vocabulary of a
major key. Which means that a diminished seventh not only
straddles four minor keys, but, to all intents and purposes,
also four major ones as well; in the case of our example the
four major keys of C, A, E♭, and F♯.

There is still one further feature of the diminished seventh to
remark upon, concerning the manner of its resolution. Hitherto
we have only seen it resolve upon the dominant seventh, the

chord of its resolution; as often as not, however (and to a lesser extent this is also true of the other dominant discords), it by-passes the dominant seventh and proceeds straight to that chord's target. Beneath the resolution to G of the appoggiatura note A♭ of a diminished seventh the other voices instead of standing still, as we have hitherto seen them doing, move to

form the common chord of C:  . In the chapter

Ex.109

above on the formation of discords (see page 54) we saw that this free treatment of an appoggiatura chord had its roots in the sixteenth-century treatment of the suspension. Such handling conferred upon the diminished seventh, armed as it was with an appoggiatura note thrusting forcefully a semitone down into the chord of the tonic, a key-establishing power almost as strong as that of the dominant seventh itself. It, too, prepared the ear for a tonality—indeed for as many as eight different possible tonalities!

I remarked above that the rootless diminished seventh had a spine-chilling ambiguity, 'as though somehow it were poised perilously on the brink of a terrifying abyss'. We can see now that this was more than a mere image. And by the same token we can see that the chord can be employed for other purposes than the expression of terror. By the simple expedient of converting its B into C♭ the diminished seventh of the key of C major could act like a magic carpet abolishing tonal space and wafting us rapidly and inevitably into the key of E♭ major:

Ex. 110

* B enharmonically converted into C♭

The one key seems to pass effortlessly into the other, to melt into it, under our eyes. There is no effect of calculated surprise —that effect which plays such a vital part in the movements of the Vienna Classics—and no effect either of calculated anticipation. There are no such effects because here the diminished seventh acts, as I said, like a magic carpet *abolishing tonal space*—abolishing, that is to say, the very dimension in which the sonata-form principle was conceived by Haydn, Mozart and Beethoven. Employed continuously, a modulation such as this one—an enharmonic modulation, to give it its technical name—could transform the chequer-board of demarcated key-relationships upon which the Vienna Classics made their moves into a kaleidoscope of keys effortlessly melting into one another. It could in fact transform the very system of tonality.

*　　*　　*　　*

At the beginning of this chapter I pointed out that, in order to understand how in the romantic idiom chromaticism transformed the key system, it would be necessary to put the dominant seventh under the microscope and study it from two points of view. Throughout the chapter we have been studying it from one point of view only, namely, that of its appoggiatura derivatives, the dominant major and minor ninths. In the romantic expressiveness of the major ninth, in the practice of 'appoggiaturing' the appoggiatura, in the enharmonic properties of the diminished seventh, we have seen tendencies making for transformation. In the next chapter, adjusting the focus of our microscope and looking at the dominant seventh from another point of view, we shall further pursue these tendencies.

SUMMARY OF CHAPTER XIV

The purpose of the penultimate chapters of this book is to show how chromaticism, which through the resource of modulation to the remote keys of chromatic triads enabled the Vienna Classics to extend the key system on a grand scale, modified and transformed the system in the romantic idiom of the nineteenth century.

In order to understand this, we must acquaint ourselves with the fact that the dominant seventh acts as the resolving chord of five appoggiatura chords: the dominant major and minor ninths, the dominant eleventh and the dominant major and minor thirteenths.

It will suffice here to concentrate attention upon the functioning of the dominant major and minor ninths.

(1) *The dominant major ninth*

The chord has in itself a bitter-sweet yearning, intrinsically 'romantic' quality.

It is frequently employed in a four-note version, the root being omitted. This omission does not impair its essential character.

In the eighteenth century the chord's expressiveness is normally kept in bounds by the unfolding rhythmic pattern of a piece. In the nineteenth century the chord underwent two developments:

    (i) Its expressiveness was given its head at the expense of the unfolding rhythmic pattern of a piece.

    (ii) It in its turn acted as the resolving chord of an appoggiatura chord, in which its bitter-sweetness became intensified to an exquisite agony.

        These developments made for a modification and transformation of the key system. In the idiom of the Vienna Classics, in which key change is the essence of the argument, the fundamental harmony of the major triad and dominant seventh pervades the themes and hence the whole texture of a work. In the romantic idiom fundamental harmony is the foundation of a superstructure of intensely expressive appoggiatura chords, which blunt the edge of the tonal argument and clog a movement's rhythmic drive.

(2) *The dominant minor ninth*

The chord has features in common with the major dominant ninth.

    (i) It is frequently employed in a four-note rootless version which does not impair its character.

    (ii) It has a bitter-sweetness of expression, which is, however, distinctively mournful.

        The expressiveness of the chord could be given its head without the deflecting of an established rhythm. It was fully exploited in the eighteenth century, notably by Bach.

    (iii) It acts as the resolving chord of an appoggiatura chord.

The chord also has distinctive features which throw light upon the romantic transformation of the key system from another point of view.

    (i) The four notes of its rootless version combine diatonically in four minor keys, e.g. C minor, A minor, E♭ minor, and F♯ minor.

   (ii) The dominant minor ninth is part of the stock vocabulary of a major key. Thus to all intents and purposes the four notes of its rootless version combine diatonically in four major keys as well, e.g. C major, A major, E♭ major, and F♯ major.

 (iii) The chord can by-pass its resolving dominant seventh and resolve directly upon the tonic. So doing it can take the place of the dominant seventh as a key-establishing chord.

> Since it is poised on the brink of as many as eight different tonalities, the rootless version of the chord has *qua* chord a spine-chilling ambiguity. Hence its employment in scenes of terror and mystery.

In virtue of its technical structure, the rootless version, the diminished seventh, is a vehicle of enharmonic modulation. This is a device which if employed continuously could transform the key system.

By enharmonically altering the B♮ of a diminished seventh in C major into a C♭ the chord becomes a diminished seventh in E♭ major. In this rapid effortless passage from C major to remote E♭ major there is no effect of surprise, nor any build-up of the remote key. The modulation acts as a magic carpet abolishing tonal space, the dimension of classical sonata-form.

CHAPTER XV

Chromaticism and the Dominant Seventh (2)

THE point of view from which in this chapter we are going to study the dominant seventh is in the context of this book entirely new. Hitherto, in all the many examples that have been given, we have seen it as the pivotal key-establishing chord exerting its thrust in the full close; we have no other idea of it. Here we are going to re-orientate ourselves: we are going to see the dominant seventh renounce its star part—the part to which it owes its very name of dominant seventh—and adopt a humbler role. This time when a foreign dominant seventh enters a key it will not, as I put it above, 'in the act of disrupting the old key set up a new one': it will be, as the chromatic triads were, *quitted* as well as approached chromatically. It will not resolve on the triad to which it thrusts, but instead be treated purely and simply as a chromatic chord. Thus, to take a very common example, the dominant seventh on the super-tonic, D—or rather, as we ought to call it when it plays this humbler role, the super-tonic chromatic seventh—instead of resolving on the major triad of G and so establishing G major, resolves back into the old key:

Ex. III

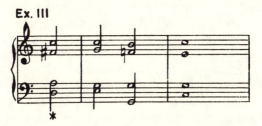

The effect of this is anything but sensational: as the dominant seventh of a related key the chord has a familiar ring; and it is resolved upon the tonic triad.

Let us consider the effect under different conditions. One of them is illustrated by another very common progression: the resolution upon the tonic triad of the erstwhile dominant seventh on the flattened sub-mediant, A♭, a dominant seventh

governing a *remote* key:  . Since it is the source of

some of the most magically beautiful effects in all music, and since it also throws further light upon the romantic tendencies discussed in the previous chapter, it will reward us to consider it more closely.

The chord evolved through the practice of adding, to a progression of the A♭ chromatic triad to the chord of the tonic,

Ex. 112

a passing note, F: and then making the

progression more forceful by inserting a chromatically shar-

Ex. 113

pened F: . The chord's name

reflects this origin: since the chromatic sharpening of F augments the interval of a major sixth between F♮ and the root A♭, it is known as an augmented sixth.[1]

F♯, however, is the same note as G♭: call it what you will, the chord is still potentially the dominant seventh—A♭–C–E♭–G♭—of the remote key of D♭. It takes us to the very brink of the remote key—and resolves back upon the tonic chord, resolves with the utmost grace and ease, melts into it. Hence the magic of the progression. It reveals a distant prospect, but, as it moves, the prospect dissolves and, as though awakening from a dream, we find ourselves at home. That unforgettable

---

[1] Augmented sixths also occur in other forms, but to describe them would take me outside the scope of this chapter. The interested reader must consult a textbook proper.

closing phrase of Schubert's song *Litanei*, I think, illustrates the magic:

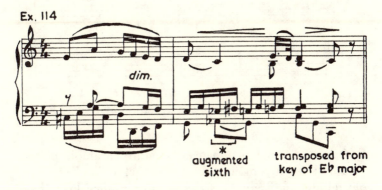

Ex. 114

augmented sixth

transposed from key of E♭ major

The pianist is compelled to linger here—as at that major ninth in the Op. 109. If we go further and, as we compared that major ninth to the one in 'Deh vieni', compare Schubert's phrase to a phrase from the first movement of the 'Eroica', we shall once again see romantic expressiveness being kept in bounds by an unfolding rhythmic pattern:

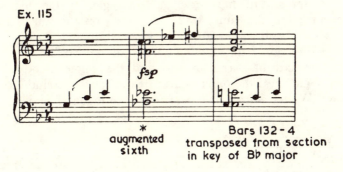

Ex. 115

augmented sixth

Bars 132-4
transposed from section in key of B♭ major

To hold back Beethoven's augmented sixth here would be unthinkable.

The fact that an augmented sixth is potentially the dominant seventh of a remote key makes it an ideal vehicle of enharmonic modulation: like the diminished seventh the chord can be used as a magic carpet transporting in a flash:

Ex.116

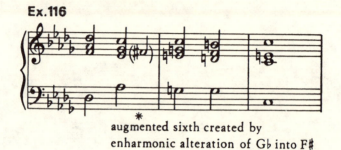

*
augmented sixth created by
enharmonic alteration of G♭ into F♯

Perhaps the supreme nineteenth-century example of such a
modulation is that moment in the first act of *The Valkyrie* when,
Siegmund and Sieglinde having discovered their love, the door
swings open and the radiance of a moonlit spring night
streams into Hunding's hut. 'Ha, who went? who entered
here?' cries Sieglinde, and Siegmund replies, 'No one went—
but one has come: laughing, the spring enters the hall.'
During this reply of Siegmund a dominant seventh, drawn out
through four whole bars and coloured with all Wagner's
mastery of ravishing orchestral effect, resolves upon the chord
of its tonic. The music swings back again to the dominant
seventh; but this time, while Siegmund on the stage 'draws
Sieglinde beside him with tender force' (I quote from Wagner's
stage-direction), the dominant seventh resolves as the augmented sixth of a remote key, and the whole mood of the
music changes: the quiet figures steal in of the prelude to the
duet 'Winter storms have waned in the moon of May':

Ex. 117

Spring   en — — ters   the

dolce

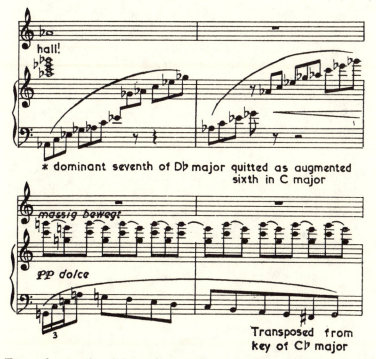

* dominant seventh of D♭ major quitted as augmented
sixth in C major

Transposed from
key of C♭ major

From the magic of the enharmonic modulation Wagner draws
dramatic poetry.

* * * *

Another way of chromatically treating a dominant seventh
is to resolve it not upon a triad, as in all the above examples,
but *upon another dominant seventh*. To take the most usual case:
the dominant seventh on D, instead of resolving as above upon
the tonic triad, resolves on the dominant seventh of the

Ex. 118

reigning key:

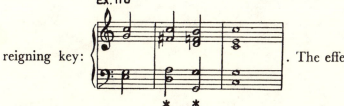

. The effect is

sweet—almost too sweet. All the same the procedure is a
highly significant one: extended chains of dominant sevenths

resolving upon each other could transform the classical key system, could convert it into a veritable whirligig of shifting tonality; as witness the four dominant sevenths in these bars from Schumann's *Er, der Herrlichste von Allen*:

Ex. 119

dominant seventh
of C major

dominant seventh
of F major

dominant seventh
of Bb major

dominant seventh
of Eb major

Bars 53-6

The succession of sweet-sounding, sharply thrusting dominant sevenths creates an effect of sentimentality: the tears flow too easily. This indeed is not one of Schumann's great songs.

*   *   *   *

The practice of resolving dominant sevenths upon each other illustrates a principle which, once we are in a position to grasp its implications, will enable us to penetrate as far as we can—

and in this book as far as we shall need to—into the arcanum of romantic harmony.

Let us start by noting that the effect of Schumann's chain of dominant sevenths is to postpone the moment of absolute resolution upon a concord. Since dominant sevenths are sweet-sounding chords their drawn-out dissonance is at any rate endurable, even though in this case their sequence is, as I said, comparable to a whirligig: swinging round from chord to chord of the same type the harmony generates no tension; it merely revolves. It is another matter if such a sequence consists not *merely* of dominant sevenths, but of dominant sevenths each preceded by an appoggiatura derivative—a dominant ninth or eleventh or thirteenth—resolving upon it. For these are chords of *different* type; and furthermore their interpolation means that the dominant sevenths are no longer directly being resolved upon each other. To put it diagrammatically: instead of

$$\text{Dominant Seventh} \dashrightarrow \text{Dominant Seventh}$$

we now have

$$\text{Appoggiatura Derivative} \rightarrow \text{Dominant Seventh} \rightarrow \text{Appoggiatura Derivative} \rightarrow \text{Dominant Seventh}$$

Before we can survey an example which will illustrate the soul-stirring possibilities of this procedure there is one final rung to climb of the ladder up which we have been struggling through these chapters on chromaticism and the dominant seventh. We must refer once more to the diminished seventh. In our examples from the Chromatic Fantasy and from *Parsifal* (see page 116) we saw the diminished seventh acting as the resolving chord of an appoggiatura derivative. We also saw that, thanks to its enharmonic structure, it potentially governs eight different tonalities. What we now have to see is the diminished seventh being treated like the dominant sevenths we have been discussing in this chapter, i.e. being resolved chromatically upon a dominant seventh. Take for example that tremendous diminished seventh, quoted above, sounded at the arrival of the Statue at Don Giovanni's banquet. Mozart does not resolve it upon the dominant seventh from which *it itself* is derived, thus:

Ex. 120

He resolves it chromatically upon another dominant seventh:[1]

Ex. 121

[1] Mozart's diminished seventh is a derivative of the dominant seventh on C minor's super-tonic, D.

The dominant seventh on D is

The dominant minor ninth on D is

The rootless diminished seventh version of the dominant minor ninth is

Mozart's arrangement of the diminished seventh is

Such chromatic treatment of this particular diminished seventh rooted on the super-tonic was standard practice throughout the eighteenth and nineteenth centuries. Not that other diminished sevenths rooted on other notes of a key were not also thus treated. But this is a matter too technical to enter into in this volume.

This final step taken, we are now in a position to survey an example in which we shall find the consummation of the romantic tendencies which we have been tracing: the opening bars of the orchestra's statement during Brangäne's song from the watch tower in the love scene of the second act of *Tristan*.

Above a tonic pedal C (the key into which I have transposed the passage—its true key is A♭ major) Wagner sounds the following series of chords:

A rootless major ninth resolving upon an inverted dominant seventh on F, C's sub-dominant:

An 'appoggiatura'd' diminished seventh resolving upon the diminished seventh rooted on G, C's dominant:

A major thirteenth resolving upon an inverted dominant seventh on C:

A rootless major ninth resolving upon an inverted dominant seventh on G, C's dominant:

An eleventh resolving upon an inverted dominant seventh on F, C's sub-dominant:

Here is the series set forth in its context, with the sequence
of appoggiaturas finally reaching a moment of absolute
resolution upon the chromatic triad of the final bar:[2]

Ex. 122

transposed from
key of A♭ major

This passage illustrates on a grand scale the two main
romantic tendencies inimical to the classical key-system, discussed above. The first was that lingering appoggiatura pathos,
which, we saw, tended to blur the clear-cut thematic statement
and clog the rhythmic drive of the classical movement in
sonata-form. The melody here is nothing but a sequence of
falling appoggiaturas, each one lingering for two whole bars
and each one, except the last, resolving upon a discord itself
requiring resolution. For all the ravishing harmonic effect of
the succession of phrases melting chromatically into each other,
the 'soul' of the music is this melodic sequence of appoggiaturas:
it is as though Wagner had marshalled his harmonies in order
to be able to pile up just this sequence, in order to be able to
vent to the full that 'psycho-physiological' pathos inherent in
the intervals of a falling tone and semitone.

The other romantic tendency is illustrated by the tonic pedal
sustained for ten bars. I said above apropos Tchaikovsky's
'appoggiatura'd' ninth that the practice of 'appoggiaturing the

---

1 In order to facilitate its reading I have not transcribed the figuration of this
passage, but reduced it to its harmonic essentials.

appoggiatura' meant that a single fundamental harmony was being sustained in order to support a superstructure growing more and more intensely expressive: and that such sustaining was inimical to classical sonata-form, animated by a logic of harmonic motion. Harmonic motion here is tethered to that pedal: each successive phrase suggests a different key, but the pedal robs the suggestion of any force. Defining a single harmony, it acts as a counterpoise to the chromatic drift of the dominant sevenths: on one plane the tonality drifts, but on another it is standing still. Whereas in the system of the Vienna Classics the business of harmony is to enact a clear-cut drama of thematic conflict, needing time in which to unfold its total effect, here its purpose is to render a few moments unforgettable, to charge a few bars with the utmost expressive eloquence.

Yet when all is said Wagner is a special case. This chapter and the last have led us to *Tristan* because there lies the arcanum of romantic harmony, there we find the romantic tendencies which we have been tracing carried to a pitch at which they transform the system of the Vienna masters. Beyond Wagner lay the post-Wagnerians—Strauss, Mahler and the rest—whom this transformation influenced, who, as we shall see, carried his tendencies to a point from which, carried a stage further, they would lead to the disintegration of his idiom in a welter of sheer chromaticism. Nevertheless, for all his great influence Wagner was, I say, a special case. For in his hands the transformation of idiom served a dramatic purpose: in *Tristan* his aim is to convey a night-world of blissful longing ('Hold us, O night!' the lovers cry, and the image pervades the whole opera)—hence the melting appoggiaturas, hence the indeterminate shifting tonality. Other nineteenth-century composers, no less romantic than Wagner— Schubert (1797–1828), Mendelssohn (1809–47), Schumann (1810–56), Chopin (1810–49), Tchaikovsky (1840–93), Dvořák (1841–1904), César Franck (1822–90), Brahms (1833–97)— wrote symphonies and sonatas in which the key system of the Vienna Classics was not so much transformed as modified. In my next chapter, to which I have given the title 'Romantic Sonata-Form', I propose to discuss some of these works—even though I run the risk of appearing to make a digression by involving myself, as I shall have to, in detailed analysis of passages from individual movements. The risk, however, must be run, since in no other way can it be made clear how a synthesis (the possibility of which Wagner denied) was achieved between classical sonata-form and the inimical tendencies of romanticism.

SUMMARY OF CHAPTER XV

The purpose of this chapter is to study the effect of the dominant seventh when it is quitted chromatically, i.e. when it is not followed by the tonic chord to which it thrusts, but by some other chord.

(1) *The chromatic resolution of the dominant seventh upon a triad*

An unsensational frequent procedure is the resolution of the erstwhile dominant seventh on D upon the tonic chord.

Another frequent procedure, the resolution of the erstwhile dominant seventh on Ab (or chord of the augmented sixth) on the tonic triad, plays a part in the romantic transformation of the key system since it is a vehicle of enharmonic modulation.

The chord owes its name of augmented sixth to the fact that it arose through the interpolation of a passing note, F♯, into a progression of the Ab triad to the chord of the tonic.

The resolution is singularly beautiful and effortless. If the chord is approached from the key of Db, of which it is the dominant seventh: Ab–C–Eb–Gb, and then, by converting the Gb into an F♯, enharmonically altered into an augmented sixth in the key of C major, it effects a rapid and easy modulation abolishing the tonal space between the two keys.

(2) *The chromatic resolution of the dominant seventh upon another dominant seventh*

A common example is the dominant seventh on the super-tonic D chromatically resolving on the dominant seventh of the reigning key. The progression of one sweet-sounding sharply thrusting dominant seventh upon another is liable to create an effect of sentimentality. A succession of such chords can convert the key system into a whirligig of shifting tonality.

(3) *The chromatic resolution of a diminished seventh upon a dominant seventh*

The example given from that of Mozart's *Don Giovanni* is that of a diminished seventh derived from the dominant seventh on the super-tonic D chromatically resolving upon the dominant seventh of the reigning key.

Both the romantic exploitation of the dominant seventh-derived appoggiatura chords studied in the previous chapter, and that of the practice, referred to in the above paragraphs, of resolving dominant sevenths upon each other and of resolving a diminished seventh upon a dominant seventh, are exemplified in a passage quoted from *Tristan*.

The melody of this passage consists of a sequence of pathetically falling appoggiaturas. Four of the appoggiatura-notes are harmonized by derivatives of the dominant seventh and resolve upon this chord; the dominant sevenths are drawn from different keys and resolve upon each other; another appoggiatura note resolves upon a diminished seventh; another upon a chromatic triad. A tonic pedal is sustained throughout for ten bars.

The succession of yearning appoggiaturas, the indeterminate shifting tonality of the dominant discords, the ravishing bitter-sweetness of their sound, the static pedal note, convey the dramatic situation: Tristan and Isolde's absorption in a night-world of blissful longing.

Whereas in the idiom of the Vienna Classics the dominant seventh is the agent of a long-term thematic conflict, here it is employed, together with its derivative appoggiatura chords, in order to charge a few bars with the utmost romantic expressive eloquence.

CHAPTER XVI

Romantic Sonata-form

In order to understand how a synthesis was achieved between classical sonata-form and the inimical tendencies of romanticism we must look beyond the sphere of harmony.

We saw above that in the idiom of the Vienna Classics key change was the dimension in which a composer's thoughts were cast. Later we saw that thinking in this dimension imposed certain conditions; that incessant enharmonic modulation abolishing tonal space would destroy the qualities of key-relationship; that themes, if they are to perform their function of implying fundamental harmonies and imparting rhythmic momentum, must not be encumbered by distractingly expressive appoggiaturas. What in this chapter we have to understand is the possibility of creating a large-scale movement which breaks these conditions and yet can still be regarded as 'in' sonata-form. To understand this we must look beyond the sphere of harmony and consider the organization of such a movement also in terms of its melody, rhythm and tone-colour.

Perhaps it lies in the nature of the case that in any detailed analysis of a masterpiece of the classical idiom pride of place tends to be given to its harmonic organization. For this organization supremely lends itself to detailed analysis: tracing the course of a work's modulations, transcribing in words the pattern of its musical structure, one is, as it were, 'explaining' it. It is a different matter when one attempts to analyse in detail a work's melodic organization. That charming opening of the 'Jupiter' development section can be 'explained' by pointing out that Mozart has put a second subject melody into the key of a flattened sub-mediant; but one cannot 'explain' why he hit upon that particular melody. True, one could say that its flowing quavers afford a contrast with the abrupt rhythms of the first subject: but this does not go very far. True, when a melody is developed from another melody the original and the development can be scrutinized and compared: but this does not 'explain' why the development should have taken that form and no other. Still less can we 'explain' (not that attempts have not been made) why a whole symphony, consisting of melodically unrelated movements, can nevertheless create an effect of unity. Analysis here is helpless: we are left open-mouthed before the miracle of the composer's melodic genius.

For all its harmonic organization a masterpiece of the classical idiom is like any other a manifestation of melodic genius. Far more is required of its melodies than merely that they should conform to the conditions I have mentioned: within their limits they must be beautiful and telling; they must set each other off; they must coalesce; they must generate new melodies. When modulation is under way they must never be mere vehicles devised for the movement of the harmony. Throughout they must take charge.

If it is true that, when all is said, it is melody—albeit of a certain kind, subject to certain conditions—which takes the centre of the stage in the sonata-form movements of the Vienna Classics, then it becomes possible to envisage another type of sonata-form movement, in which another kind of melody takes the centre of the stage under different conditions.

For example, compare the first subject of the first movement of Schubert's 'Unfinished' to that of the 'Jupiter'. Mozart's subject is dominated by a brief incisive theme manifestly designed with an eye to its subsequent symphonic development (see Example 82, page 99). Schubert's contains two themes: the first like Mozart's a brief incisive affair earmarked for development, and the second an extended theme of *lyrical* character, i.e. a theme conceived in terms of the inflexions of the voice, a self-contained song without words unfolding in a succession of balanced phrases, rising to a climax:

Ex. 123

Bars 13 - 19

How this extended lyrical theme of his first subject causes
Schubert to modify the classical treatment of sonata-form can
be seen in his management of the bridge passage immediately
following the above example. Mozart's bridge passage, we saw,
was an elaborate affair, building up the tonal system of the
new key and at the same time decisively advancing the thematic
argument. Schubert, on the other hand, after his lyrical
outburst relaxes. He has up his sleeve another extended lyrical
melody for his second subject, which will form a striking
contrast with that of his first. If the contrast is to take effect he
cannot spend time building up the new tonal system: he must
reach his new key as quickly and unobtrusively as he can.
And so he contents himself with these four peremptory bars:

Ex. 124

For a logic of harmonic argument Schubert is substituting here
a logic of melodic contrast.

In the development section of this movement we again see a
logic of sheer melody, if not actually substituted for, at any rate
modifying the classic harmonic logic. The scope of the modulation is very restricted, compared to that of the 'Jupiter':
instead of the elaborate interplay of a number of themes
conducted over a whole range of related and remote keys,
Schubert stays nearly all the time within the tonal system of his
home key and develops one theme only, namely the opening
six bars of the movement:

Ex. 125

And yet the development is tremendous—thanks to the
expressive power which Schubert wrings from the phrase, and

to the scoring (which we shall discuss below). In this, the first of the romantic symphonies, we find Schubert showing Wagner how to exploit the highly charged pathos of the dominant discord by writing the kind of melody that demands it. Thus he trans-

poses his opening figure :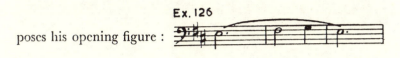

inverts this transposition : ,

combines the two:  and

adds to the combination the dominant triad, F♯–A♯–C♯, of his home key, B minor:

Bars 139-41

Together with this triad the G and the E of the two figures form

the five-note chord of a minor dominant ninth:

Schubert elaborates the chord he has thus created for eleven whole bars:

Ex. 130

Bars 139-151

What with the quickening rhythm of the melody, coiling and uncoiling, straining to resolve, and the thickening orchestration and the growing volume, the passage has great force. Although in the context of the development section as a whole it forms part of a harmonic design, a restricted one, modelled on the Vienna Classics, in itself the passage can be regarded as the very prototype of romantic expression. Schubert here is conveying the lesson applied so thoroughly in *Tristan*: is showing Wagner how to charge a few bars with the utmost eloquence.

              *   *   *   *

Let us now consider the first movement of the 'Unfinished' from the point of view of its rhythm and tone-colour.

I remarked above that had Beethoven encumbered symphonic themes with distractingly expressive appoggiaturas he would have clogged the rhythmic drive of his movements. To linger over an appoggiatura is to pull it out of its context and draw attention to it as an item of special significance. But in the classical movement in sonata-form every item is subordinate to the total effect created by its tightly knit harmonic logic. Every item, therefore, is embedded in its context: pull it out and you destroy the organism. All such movements accordingly have to be harnessed to a single tempo, to which every rhythmic pattern must conform; the tempo may give here and there, but in the performance which realizes the full stature of the work it never relaxes its grip, never fails to stamp its character on the movement as a whole.

Schubert's movement, however, as we have just seen, is knit not only by harmonic argument but by a logic of melody. Its rhythmic structure is accordingly looser—as witness that bridge passage where, after the lyrical outburst of his first subject, he relaxes. Literally he relaxes: during those peremptory four bars of modulation a note is tied for two bars bringing the rhythmic flow of the music to a complete stop. Thus Schubert's second subject which, we saw, has no harmonic build-up, has no rhythmic build-up either. Whereas in the 'Jupiter' Mozart heralds the arrival of his second subject with a strenuous bridge passage culminating in a succession of loud crotchet chords decorated by whirling demisemiquavers, Schubert clears his stage abruptly and leaves it to his second subject to sidle quietly on and ingratiate itself as best it can.

That in the event the subject does ingratiate itself is due not only to its intrinsic lyrical charm, nor to the melodic contrast that it brings, but to its tone-colour—and to the tone-colour of all that has gone before.

If one were so foolhardy as to attempt to define in a single sentence the difference between the classical and the romantic outlook one might do worse than say that the former is more instinctively concerned with the over-all total effect, the latter with the immediate, momentary one. Thus while the business of classical harmony is to enact a large-scale drama of thematic conflict, the romantic harmony of *Tristan* aims at overwhelming us here and now. Similarly with tone-colour: to the classic composer the orchestra broadly speaking is as a rule no more than the apt and telling servant of his design; to the romantic the orchestra is a veritable genie enabling a single thought to transcend itself: not merely to stir us immediately by its eloquent pathos, but to throw us as well into a stage of sensuous rapture, to enchant and intoxicate us. Those *Tristan* appoggiatura chords in their orchestral setting—delicately articulated by harps across a soft background of sustained woodwind blended with gently syncopated strings—not only move us by their pathos, but overwhelm us with the sheer ravishing beauty of their sound.

Schubert's orchestra, too, is a genie. The haunting beauty of his lyrical first subject theme is bound up with the tone of the oboe delivering it above the restless accompanying figure of the strings. The ingratiating charm of the second subject—and the melodic contrast that it brings—is bound up with the tone of the cello delivering the melody—of the cello now, not the oboe. The tremendous power of that passage in the development section discussed above is bound up with the thickening orchestration, above all with the throbbing *sforzatos* of Schubert's three trombones, first syncopated, then pounding out a series of hammer blows:

Ex. 131

Bars 139-151

*   *   *   *

Of the first movement of Schubert's 'Unfinished' it could be said broadly that it achieves a synthesis between classical sonata-form and the tendencies of romanticism in that it reduces the role of modulation and exploits that of melodic contrast reinforced by tone-colour. Let us now consider to what extent this can be said of the two other foremost symphonists of the nineteenth century, Brahms and Tchaikovsky.

Let us take Tchaikovsky's greatest achievement, the first movement of the 'Pathétique'. Here we find the recapitulation of the classical sonata-form drastically modified. Whereas Schubert after the excitement of his development section settles down unperturbed to write a recapitulation to all intents and purposes exact, Tchaikovsky, as he approaches the bridge passage leading to the return of the second subject, turns aside to deliver the most shattering of the movement's many shattering outbursts, an outburst raising the restless despair of the first subject and development section to a pitch of almost hysterical frenzy. After this the second subject is a ghost of its former self: its former expression-mark 'teneramente, molto cantabile, con espansione' is now 'con dolezza'; the figure of a chromatic scale winds sadly through it, it is curtailed, attenuated. Such a recapitulation is indeed a drastic departure from the essential 'A–B–A' ternary principle of the classical design; it is as though the sheer unrestrained violence of Tchaikovsky's outburst had brought him to a point of no return. Schubert for all the excitement of his development section could restore the previous situation—but for Tchaikovsky the china has been smashed and there is nothing left but to pick up the pieces and mourn their loss.

The outburst itself is conducted by means of that same apparatus of romantic harmony which we studied in the last two chapters: by means of 'psycho-physiological' appoggiaturas, a sequence of dominant discords, an enharmonically treated diminished seventh, a pedal—sustained here for as many as thirty-eight bars. The shattering impact of the passage is partly due to the force of its rhythm: to the steady crotchet and dotted crotchet tread of trumpet and tuba stamping out a scale in contrary motion; to the diminished seventh upon which the scale converges, hurled forth in a series of breath-taking syncopations:

Ex. 132

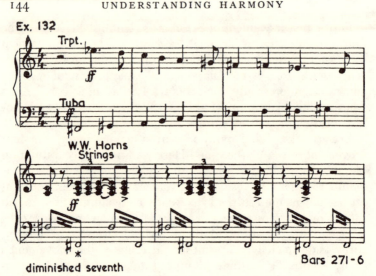

diminished seventh

Bars 271-6

As the diminished seventh resolves, the body of strings begin a series of appoggiaturas restoring the rhythmic balance of the passage: a steady pulse takes charge again, controlling the movement of each voice:

Ex. 133

Bars 277-80

The great power of the passage is, of course, also due to Tchaikovsky's orchestration. As the first subject of the 'Unfinished' is bound up with the sound of the oboe delivering it above the accompaniment of the strings, so here the effect is bound up with the sheer brute volume of tone which trumpet and tuba together produce as they stamp out their scale—and with the sheer tonal contrast between that kind of sound and the other kind—more nervous, more intense—which the body of strings produce when 'sempre ff' they launch their series of appoggiaturas.

Whether Tchaikovsky's violation of the ternary principle in

this passage should be regarded only as a modification, however drastic, of the classic design, or as amounting to a complete transformation of it, is hard to decide. The fact that Tchaikovsky elsewhere preserves the conventional scheme—that his exposition contains the normal build-up of a second subject cast in the conventional key of the relative major, and that in the development section he modulates far and wide—and the fact that anyhow the point which he chooses for his outburst is the recapitulated bridge passage, where it was classic practice to take advantage of the need to alter the course of the modulation and introduce some piece of fresh development, argues for regarding it as only a modification. But to leave it at that is to overlook the profoundly different effect which the movement as a whole makes from that of the 'Unfinished', let alone the 'Jupiter'. Tchaikovsky, so it seems to me, has here brilliantly turned to account his romantic love of the overpowering immediate effect: preserving the classic framework he has so manipulated his material that in the event it seems to build up cumulatively to that one supreme climax, shattering in its immediate effect, yet determined by all that has gone before and determining all that is to come after. In his own way (which incidentally has much in common with the way of Wagner in many of his great set pieces, of Chopin in his large-scale works, of Brahms in his slow movements) and at his own level Tchaikovsky achieves a synthesis. Spiritually no doubt the level is less edifying than that of Beethoven's Fifth— Beethoven 'takes Fate by the throat', Tchaikovsky weeps and tears his hair—but it is not less a synthesis for that, but only different. Nor, with due respect to Beethoven, need we assume with so many of Tchaikovsky's critics (out of unconscious squeamishness, I wonder?) that the level of his achievement is relatively so low. Only a great genius could expose his inner self as Tchaikovsky does here, could voice in music the dark night of the soul—the longings, the nerve storms, and the ultimate exhausted tranquillity.

*   *   *   *

Finally let us briefly consider a movement of Brahms. Brahms is a composer who, like Gaul, can be usefully divided into three parts. First there is the predominantly romantic

Brahms of the songs and slow movements, the Brahms whose yearning melodies time and time again soar to a heartrending climax of appoggiatura melody and dominant-discordant harmony; the Brahms of these bars from the slow movement of the Third Symphony:

Ex. 134

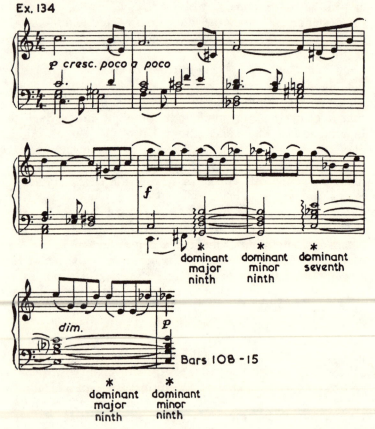

Secondly there is the predominantly classical Brahms of the outer movements of the First Symphony ('the Tenth', as Brahms's admirers nicknamed it) with their concise unlyrical subjects, their driving rhythm, their clear-cut logic of harmonic motion, the unromantic sense they convey of purposefulness and spiritual victory. Thirdly there is the Brahms with whom we must occupy ourselves here, who attempted, some would say not always successfully, to harness the inimical tendencies of romanticism to the classic pattern: the Brahms, for example, of the first movement of the Third Symphony.

It is illuminating to compare the bridge passage of this movement with that of the 'Unfinished', which we discussed above. Schubert's, we saw, is a peremptory affair: he relies on contrast of melody and tone-colour to bind his extended lyrical first and second subjects. Brahms's two subjects are also extended and lyrical and they also contrast with each other:

On the other hand the bridge passage, occupying twenty-one bars, is on the face of it anything but peremptory. The first seven bars are given to a lyrical theme, still in the key of the tonic, F major:

Brahms then transposes this theme into the remote key of D♭ major. Had it been his intention to build up the key of his second subject, A major, in the classical manner Brahms might at this point have reflected that (i) D♭ major is the enharmonic equivalent of C♯ major, (ii) C♯ major falls within the tonal system of F♯ minor, (iii) F♯ minor falls within the tonal system of A major, and accordingly built up an extended modulation. Instead he by-passes F♯ minor altogether and, with a peremp-

toriness equalling Schubert's, proceeds straight from D♭ major
into A major, thus:

Ex. 137

*
dominant seventh
of A major   Bars 29-30

In the immediacy of its effect, in the sense of surprise which the
sudden melting of D♭ major into A major evokes, this passage
is typically romantic. But Brahms needed time in which to
prepare it, had to saturate us with seven bars of D♭ major,
and the time thus taken blunts the force of the melodic contrast,
so strong in the 'Unfinished', between first and second subject.

But to drag a passage out of its context and disparage it
for not achieving what a comparable passage in another
context achieves is dangerous criticism. Obviously if we are to
do justice to Brahms we must look further and examine other
aspects of the movement's structure.

Above all it is the development section here which throws
light on the unique quality of Brahms's mind. Schubert's and
Tchaikovsky's are dominated by a single phrase, in both cases
the opening phrase of the movement; Brahms's on the other
hand is a remoulding of almost the whole material of the
exposition. Thus he starts by converting the *grazioso* second
subject (see Ex. 135) into an *agitato* cello melody in C♯ minor:

Ex. 138

agitato

ben marc.   Bars 77 - 81

This stormy melody leads back to the opening fanfare of the
movement, not, however, in its original form:

Ex. 139

Bars 1-3

but drawn out to form a solemn, lyrical phrase, delivered by the horn first in E♭, then in G♭ major:

Ex. 140

Bars 101-8

The phrase, which in its original form as a fanfare had launched the *passionato* melody of the first subject (see Ex. 135), now launches it again in remote E♭ minor. The *passionato* melody takes on here the quality of a mysterious funeral march:

Ex. 141

Bars 112-13

Suddenly the development section is over: the funeral march has led back to the beginning of the movement, the fanfare is trumpeted forth in its original form and the *passionato* melody unleashed in all its former glory.

This development section, I said, throws light on the unique quality of Brahms's mind. Its subject-matter is not a single idea, pursued and magnified, but melodic contrast created by the juxtaposing of several ideas. This being so we can perhaps see why in his exposition Brahms was not concerned, as Schubert evidently was, to point the contrast between his first and second subject: he was holding his fire in view of events to come.

Again Brahms's development section differs significantly from Schubert's and Tchaikovsky's in respect of its orchestration. Tone-colour, we saw, played a decisive part in the pursuit and magnifying of their single idea. But here there is no single idea for the orchestra to seize upon and shatter us with. Here the orchestra—and this is true of Brahms generally—is no longer the genie, but rather, as it was for the Vienna Classics, the apt and telling servant of the design as a whole.

And yet this development section differs just as profoundly from one of Mozart or Haydn or Beethoven. Take that *agitato* C♯ minor version of the *grazioso* second subject (Ex. 138). It is a 'development', the melody is derived, and yet in the event the original is transformed out of all immediate recognition. In the classical development section we never cease to feel that we are listening to an argument built upon a proposition previously stated; in these bars of Brahms we are being moved by yet another eloquent lyrical melody. We need the musical analyst to point out the derivation, to grasp which is to experience the music as something more than just a succession of separately eloquent ideas.

Even today there are some who contend that intrinsically this movement of Brahms, not to mention others, is no more than just this: that Brahms made the mistake of stretching a fundamentally limited lyrical talent upon the 'procrustean bed' (the favourite way of putting it) of sonata-form. To which one could retort that Brahms needed the ample framework of this form in which to deploy his extraordinary melodic genius; and that if this and other movements of his lack the firm clear-cut outline of the classic masterpieces, it does not follow that they fail to build up a cumulative effect in their own way.

How different the way of Brahms is from that of the classics the coda of this movement fully reveals. The *passionato* first subject flares up for the last time, more fierily than ever, and then, its energy spent, brings the movement to a quiet close. The penultimate flare-up, the quiet close—this resembles the way of Tchaikovsky. But the thoughts of Brahms and the emotions informing them are much more complex and subtle. Like the Viennese masters Brahms has an elasticity, a detachment enabling him within the compass of a single movement to pass through a whole range of moods. But here he does not pass through them in order, like Beethoven in the *Eroica*, to raise at the end a mighty bonfire in joy and thanksgiving. He does not, for, so his coda tells us, he is at heart like Tchaikovsky a disillusioned romantic. Herein his uniqueness—and herein perhaps the reason why this side of Brahms means so very much to those who love him. Not until he has fought his battles does he admit the necessity of defeat.

SUMMARY OF CHAPTER XVI

The purpose of this chapter is to understand, through analysis of works of Schubert, Tchaikovsky, and Brahms, how in the nineteenth century large-scale symphonic movements were constructed, which effected a synthesis between classical sonata-form and the inimical tendencies of romanticism.

Although key change is the dimension in which the masterpieces of the Vienna Classics were conceived, their music is at the same time a manifestation of melodic genius, working within the limits imposed by their harmonic pattern. In the romantic symphony melody works in different forms and under different conditions, modifying the classical harmonic pattern.

(1) *The first movement of Schubert's 'Unfinished' Symphony*

In order to point the melodic contrast between the lyrical portion of the first subject and the lyrical second subject Schubert modulates quickly into the key of the latter, instead of gradually building it up in the classical manner.

In the development section the range of modulation is comparatively restricted. Schubert develops by drawing on the expressive power of the 'appoggiatura'd' dominant discord.

Since Schubert is fundamentally concerned with melodic expressiveness and melodic contrast his rhythmic structure is less tightly knit than that of the Vienna Classics.

The orchestra, which for the Vienna Classics was the servant of the design as a whole, is for Schubert, and the romantics generally, a genie, imparting to single ideas a transcendent power and eloquence. Thus the force of the melodic contrast of his first and second subject and of his development section is bound up with their orchestration.

(2) *The first movement of Tchaikovsky's 'Pathétique' Symphony*

The movement contains an overpowering climax, occurring at the recapitulated bridge passage. The recapitulation of the second subject, following this climax, is so curtailed and its character so altered that it amounts to a modification of the essential ternary principle of classical sonata-form.

The climax is effected by means of appoggiaturas, a sequence of dominant discords, an enharmonically treated diminished seventh and a pedal. The trombones and tubas of Tchaikovsky's orchestra powerfully contribute to it.

(3) *The first movement of Brahms's Third Symphony*

As in the 'Unfinished', the first and second subjects are lyrical and contrast melodically. Unlike Schubert, however, Brahms does not write a short bridge passage in order to point this contrast. But neither does he build up the key of the second subject in the classical manner: he enters it by means of a characteristically romantic enharmonic modulation.

The development section, unlike that of Schubert and Tchaikovsky, is not dominated by a single idea, but re-casts the whole material of the exposition. The lyrical first and second subjects take other lyrical forms, which are effectively juxtaposed. This suggests that Brahms, in not pointing the melodic contrast of his first and second subjects, was holding his fire in view of events to come.

The development section modulates widely, but differs from the classical section in that its ideas are lyrical and in that their source in the exposition is less obviously apparent. To the criticism that sonata-form was an unsuitable vehicle for Brahms it could be retorted that he needed its ample framework for the deployment of his extraordinary melodic genius.

Brahms's affinity with the Vienna Classics is evident in his restrained use of the orchestra. On the other hand his affinity with romanticism is evident in the quiet disillusionment of the coda.

CHAPTER XVII

Some Trends of Early Twentieth-century Harmony

WHEN we come to consider harmony in the twentieth century the term can no longer be used, as it has been throughout this book, to denote a single body of harmonic principles underlying the practice of composers generally. 'Harmony' now becomes a collective term, denoting a number of diverse systems and trends. The single river which flowed through the eighteenth and nineteenth centuries has, as it were, forked out into a delta of separate streams and currents: post-Wagnerian romantic harmony, impressionism, contrapuntalism, bitonality. And this is not all: beside the delta flow other independent rivers. On the one hand neo-modalism, flowing like classical harmony from the source of folk-song; on the other hand the rivers (which some might prefer to call artificial canals) whose source lies in the twentieth century itself, e.g. the constructions of Schoenberg's twelve-note system and of Hindemith's harmony. Sometimes a single one of these streams completely informs the idiom of a composer—thus Richard Strauss is nothing but a post-Wagnerian romantic—but more often than not they interconnect with and feed each other. Thus contrapuntalism informs the utterly different harmonic styles of Schoenberg and Hindemith. Thus post-Wagnerian romanticism, impressionism, contrapuntalism, bitonality, and neo-modalism are all found mingled in the idiom of Bartók.

Between them the above-mentioned trends embody those features which are, I think, generally recognized as the most important and characteristic of twentieth-century harmony. Even so, the survey of them which I am about to make will, I fear, be anything but exhaustive. I shall have to ignore many important and significant composers and concentrate only upon a few in whom the above trends can be discerned most readily. I shall have to deal only incidentally with topics such as polytonality (as distinct from bitonality), poly-modalism and neo-classicism. This is the final portion of my book, and to deal with the harmony of the twentieth century in the detail with which I have discussed classical harmony would demand not a portion of a book, nor even a complete one, but a whole array of books.

*   *   *   *

Post-Wagnerian Romantic Harmony

Notable representatives of this trend are among others Richard Strauss (1864–1949), Mahler (1860–1911), Wolf (1860–1903), Puccini (1858–1924) and in this country Elgar (1857–1934), Delius (1862–1934), and, one might add, the Walton of the Viola Concerto and the lyrical passages of *Troilus and Cressida*. Its basis is the romantic harmony discussed in the previous chapters. We saw that a general characteristic of this harmony was its chromaticism, blurring the clear-cut sense of key which underpinned the structure of classical sonata-form. Thus we saw Wagner in *Tristan* build up a whole sequence of dominant discords resolving chromatically upon each other. We saw, too, the vital part played in the formation of these discords by the appoggiatura, the supreme agent of intense pathetic expression.

In the post-Wagnerian romantic idiom the tendencies of *Tristan* are employed in a still more wholesale fashion. Take, for example, the following passage from *The Dream of Gerontius*:

Ex. 142

The chromatically quitted E♭ and D♭ triads of the first two bars represent a typical feature. In our *Tristan* example we saw Wagner building up a drifting succession of chromatically quitted dominant sevenths: here we see Elgar employing *triads themselves*, the pillars of tonality, to create an effect of drift. Typical also is the poignant appoggiatura chord under the 'me' of the 'meus' of the fourth bar. Like the dominant ninths, elevenths, and thirteenths which we studied above the chord resolves upon a dominant seventh (here E♭–G–D♭); but now the interval between appoggiatura note (D) and root of dominant seventh (E♭) is the acutely dissonant major seventh. The continuous drift of the tonality in *Gerontius*, and the continuous poignancy of its dissonance, have everything to do with the work's indefinable atmosphere of anguished mysticism.

Another illuminating example is provided by the thrilling phrase with which Strauss builds up the climax of *Death and Transfiguration*. Stripped of the appoggiatura and passing chords and of the inessential notes—in which, of course, the whole power of the phrase lies—the fundamental harmony reveals itself as that of an E major triad sustained for two bars and succeeded by a diminished seventh:

Ex. 143

Above the triad, which in Strauss's score is delivered in the form of a series of arpeggios by the harps, the strings weave a stormily syncopated melody, which finally flings itself upon the diminished seventh:

Ex. 144

In the first two bars the melody is cluttering the triad with an appoggiaturing A, and with an inessential F♯ and E♭. At the third bar, at which it 'flings itself' upon the diminished seventh, it executes another appoggiatura, one of the same brand as those agonized appoggiatura'd diminished sevenths of our examples above from the Chromatic Fantasy and *Parsifal* (see page 116).

Meanwhile the trombones have been screwing up the tension still further. Beneath the triad they have been delivering a series of accented minims striding down the chromatic scale from E. When at the third bar they at length reach the diminished seventh they . . . but let us see for ourselves:

Ex. 145

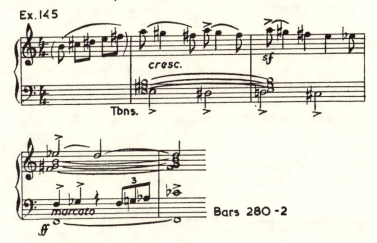

Bars 280-2

The D♯ of the trombones converts the E major triad into a passing chord; their D♮ into an inverted dominant seventh; their C♯ into—into a what? Had their scale stepped on down to the B below the C♯ it would have formed a passing chord; but the B of the diminished seventh is taken by other instruments at a higher register. The trombones instead go to F, and not content merely to stay there, deliver a sinister *marcato* flourish, darkening still further the dark harmony of the appoggiatura'd diminished seventh.[1]

The wealth of all this accumulated dissonance is typically post-Wagnerian. It is post-*Wagnerian*, since, as this example shows, despite the apparent complexity, the fundamental harmonies underlying it are still the basic traditional ones.

---

[1] Not that even this is the whole story. At the second bar Strauss sets his horns off on a scale of three minims: E, F♯, G♯, of which the F♯ coincides with the trombones' C♯. This, of course, still further complicates the dissonance: on the other hand the passage of the F♯ to the G♯ of the diminished seventh does to some extent serve to cement the chord into the context as a passing chord.

But though this is so, the passage also points away from traditional harmony to future developments, to the idioms, which we shall be discussing below, in which discords have lost their familiar bearings and of which the tonality is no longer firmly ruled and ordered by the dominant seventh.

Impressionism

An instructive comparison can be drawn between the aims of impressionism and those of romanticism. The romantic, we saw, is instinctively concerned with immediate momentary effects, rather than with the long-term structural effect of a work as a whole. Likewise the impressionist. But the immediate momentary effect which the impressionist seeks is of a different kind. Both set out to ravish the senses with a magical paraphernalia of chromatic transition, bitter-sweet dissonance and instrumental tone-colour, but to the romantic this paraphernalia is a means to an end: he is reaching through the senses to the heart, using every resource to wring and overwhelm us with the pathetic intensity of his utterance. The impressionist stops short at the senses. Not because he is emotionless, but because he abhors what Debussy (1862–1918) called the 'professional rhetoric' of romantic eloquence. He prefers to rejoice quietly in chordal sonority and tone-colour for their own sake and for that of the subtle evocations of nature they can convey. In the romantic idiom melody, the agent of emotional expression, always has priority—as witness those appoggiaturas of our *Tristan* example. In the impressionist idiom melody is rather the instrument of harmonic and tone-colouristic effect. The melody of Debussy's *L'Après-midi d'un faune*, for example, is a filigree of short phrases of uneven length and fluctuating tempo, designed not to build up cumulatively to a climax, but rather through their very disparateness to pin-point one by one a succession of ravishing harmonic and orchestral effects. Only in the middle section of the work does melody take wing and the voice of romantic passion disturb the peace of the drowsy afternoon.

In order to obtain an idea of the technique of impressionism, and of its specifically 'modern' feature, the practice of leaving discords unresolved, it will suffice here if we concentrate upon the role played therein by the time-honoured device of the pedal. A further reason for devoting some paragraphs to this topic—even at the risk of appearing to make a digression—is that the device of the pedal, apart from its value to the impressionist, has played an important part in twentieth-century harmony generally. Thus, as I shall show later, it is the source of the trend of bitonality.

We saw above (see page 57) that a pedal is a note sustained throughout a harmonization regardless of the discords thereby formed. We saw that when the pedal was the tonic sustained in the bass the discords it produced were innocuous, that the individual quality of each chord of a harmonization was unimpaired, but that the effect of the pedal was to tether a progression to the tonic and weaken the sense of departure which constitutes the essence of the logic of tonality. It remains to add here that if the pedal is sustained by another note than the tonic then the sheer fact of its being continuously sounded will tend to establish it as one, so potent is its effect. From the point of view of the twentieth-century composer seeking an alternative to the classical method of establishing a tonic by means of the dominant seventh, this power of the pedal has important possibilities. It enables him to set up a series of tonal centres, as it were, by brute force, at the same time leaving him free—since a pedal does not impair the individual quality of the chords above—to weave an individual harmonic texture, atonal, contrapuntal, neo-modal, impressionist or otherwise. Already in our *Tristan* example we have seen Wagner employing a pedal note to underpin a sequence of discords. In Walton's Symphony and in the symphonies of Sibelius and of Vaughan Williams and in the quartets of Bartók the pedal has a similar structural role.

But there is more to the pedal than even this. The chordal combination which it produces of a cluster of dissonant upper notes placed high above a fundamental can convey a specific inherently attractive sensuous effect—presumably because its pattern broadly corresponds with the natural pattern of the harmonic series, the upper reaches of which contain overtones clashing with the bass of the fundamental. If the dissonant upper overtone-notes of such a chord, which in nature are weak, are not treated as appoggiaturas demanding to be stressed, but sounded gently, then the discord—for all the fact that it is a discord—has a mysteriously cool, emotionless, and yet at the same time vaguely evocative quality, which makes it the ideal vehicle of impressionism—as witness the still silent sea evoked in Debussy's *La Cathédrale engloutie*:

Ex. 146

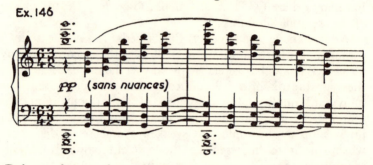

Debussy leaves these discords unresolved. Not out of mere antagonism to the 'professional rhetoric' of romanticism, but because to have resolved them would have spoilt their artistic effect: their evocation of the aloof inhuman sea. Nevertheless, the procedure was revolutionary, for it meant that the discord, traditionally treated as a chord of tension demanding resolution, was setting itself up as a chord of repose. Inherently it was more revolutionary than the post-Wagnerian romantic harmony of our Strauss example which, far from treating the discord as a chord of repose, exploited its tension to the utmost lengths. Debussy, the founder of impressionism, only exploited the device intermittently; it was left to others to follow the path which he laid open and attempt a wholesale transvaluation of the traditional values of harmony.

Contrapuntalism

Early in this book I pointed out that music is experienced simultaneously both upon a vertical and upon a horizontal plane, and that the relative vividness of the two depended on the style of a work. Thus we saw that Bach's style was primarily horizontal: his tendency was to eschew harmonic effects for their own sake and to rely upon the logic of his counterpoint to reconcile the ear to the dissonance and chromaticism which it produced. The twentieth-century trend of contrapuntalism stems from Bach. Bach invested heavily in counterpoint and drew a rich dividend. The twentieth-century composer, oppressed by the lush sensuousness and highly charged emotionalism of romantic harmony, divests himself of this legacy and looks back to the more austere, more intellectual Bach. As, by the virtue of his contrapuntal logic, Bach reconciled the ear to dissonance and chromaticism, so, by the virtue of his, could the composer today reconcile the ear to harmony purged of the too-familiar overwhelming associations of the past.

I remarked above that the trend of contrapuntalism is one which informs the styles of composers otherwise utterly different from each other, and as an example of this cited Schoenberg and Hindemith. I might also have cited the neo-classic style of Stravinsky—of, for instance, the ballet *Apollo Musagetes*, in which Stravinsky can be seen 'going back to Bach' (as the phrase goes) most whole-heartedly: dispensing with the vast orchestral apparatus of the post-Wagnerian romantics and scoring for strings only; adopting the form of the Bach suite and the style of Bach's ornamentation; relying on a limpid clear-cut counterpoint to justify the harmonic liberties he takes.[1] Again contrapuntalism is an important element in the eclectic style of Bartók. As witness this passage from the cadenza of the Violin Concerto:

Ex. 147

1st movement, bars 344 - 8

---

[1] In other neo-classic works of his, Stravinsky has 'gone back' to other composers than Bach: thus to Pergolesi in *Pulcinella*, to Tchaikovsky in *The Fairy's Kiss* and to Mozart in *The Rake's Progress*.

The two voices, the upper one polarized around A♭, the lower one round B♭, produce an acutely dissonant harmony, and reconcile us to it by the logic of the canonic counterpoint they weave. But at the vivace the A♭–B♭ discord gives way to a resolving A♮ octave: acute and long drawn out though it is, the dissonance of this counterpoint of Bartók's has not, like Schoenberg's, severed all connexion with the moorings of traditional harmony.

Bitonality

Bitonality is the simultaneous combining of two keys, polytonality of more than two. Since the use of polytonality has never been widespread—its chief exponent is Milhaud and he has more or less abandoned it in recent years—I shall deal here only with bitonality, which is on the contrary one of the most ubiquitous and fruitful of twentieth-century harmonic developments.[1]

I remarked above that the source of bitonality was the time-honoured device of the pedal. That this is so is evident from the fact, already commented upon, that the sounding of a pedal leaves unimpaired the individual quality of the chords of a progression. If the second phrase of the National Anthem executes its cadential change to the key of A minor above a tonic pedal:

Ex. 148

Cadential change
to A minor above tonic pedal

we experience the key change even though the continuously sounding tonic is tethering the tonality of the piece to C major. We experience in fact two simultaneously heard tonal centres—

[1] The reader interested in particulars of polytonality is referred to the chapter on that subject in Humphrey Searle's *Twentieth-Century Counterpoint*.

yet another example of that power of 'selective awareness', which, as we saw, enables us to disentangle horizontal from vertical impressions and give to each their due as the context dictates.

Another device, closely related to the pedal and even more time-honoured (it can be traced back to the very beginnings of music), has an important bearing upon the development of bitonality: the primitive device of continually repeating a single short figure at the same pitch. As, for example, this figure, which in the Finale of Sibelius's Second Symphony winds its way through nearly seventy bars:

Ex. 149

A so-called ostinato figure such as this, continually revolving around a tonic note, can underpin a harmonic progression no less efficiently than the sustaining of a pedal (as witness the tremendous effect of that ostinato of Sibelius, the sense it creates of being chained inexorably to the key of D minor). When the ostinato ceases to be a mere supporting figure, revolving around the tonic, and becomes a fully fledged idea in its own right the step to bitonality is taken.

Stravinsky's early neo-primitive masterpiece, *The Rite of Spring*, contains striking instances of bitonality. Thus in the following example the G♯ minor melody, delivered by muted trumpets, is combined with a B♭ major sixth, reiterated by bassoons and decorated by a bass flute with a winding chromatic figure:

Ex. 150

"Action Rituelle des Ancêtres" 132

The extreme simplicity of the two ideas and the sharp contrast of their tone-colouring make it easy enough to disentangle them as two separate horizontal trains of thought. Thus for all that the reckless clashing of the two keys is eloquently expressive of the wild barbaric rite which is the music's subject-matter, the total effect is still not one of chaos. The horizontal impression is paramount.

Examples of a more subtle use of bitonality occur in the music of Benjamin Britten. Thus in the orchestral interlude depicting the storm in *Peter Grimes* the savage wind's madcap frolic in E♭ major:

Ex. 151

is given a diabolical edge by a fortissimo accompaniment of D major tonic and dominant chords. The passage lasts for eighteen bars and it serves a structural as well as a pictorial purpose. The interlude as a whole has the design of a rondo in E♭ minor, with two episodes in other keys, of which the latter is this bitonal passage. Hard on its heels comes the return of the main E♭ minor section, its tearing impact magnificently enhanced by the fact that it is putting an end to the prolonged dissonance of those eighteen bitonal bars and at last establishing a single unequivocal key. Indeed this establishing is to all intents and purposes a classical gesture: it denotes the classical attitude towards dissonance as a state of tension due to be resolved. That Britten in this bitonal context makes this gesture, and with such magnificent effect, goes to show what riches an inventive contemporary mind can still draw from the heritage of the traditional idiom.

Neo-modalism

In the opening paragraph of this chapter I referred to neo-modalism as an independent river flowing, like classical harmony, out of the pool of folk-song. The medieval modes, of which the Ionian and Aeolian were the source of classical harmony, providing as they did the harmonic cadences of a key system, were probably originally drawn from folk-song. Apart from the Ionian and Aeolian, the most ubiquitous have been the Mixolydian, the Lydian, the Dorian, and the Phrygian. The first two of these resemble the major scale, the Mixolydian, as we saw, having a flattened leading-note:

Ex. 152

and the Lydian a sharpened sub-dominant:

Ex. 153

The other two are like the melodic minor, the Dorian resembling the ascending version with a flattened leading-note:

Ex. 154

and the Phrygian the descending version with a flattened supertonic:

Ex. 155

Apart from the modes, the so-called pentatonic scale of five notes (C, D, E, G, A) was widely employed in various forms in the folk-songs of Europe and beyond, while outside Europe there, of course, existed an immense variety.

Already in the nineteenth century the Ionian-Aeolian hegemony was beginning to show some signs of cracking: 'modal' (by which is meant: 'other-than-major-and-minor-modal') melodies were playing a part in the idiom of Chopin (1810–49), Dvořák (1841–1904), Moussorgsky (1839–81), Grieg (1843–1907), and other non-German composers. This revolt was partly a matter of racial musical instinct, partly a cultural revolt against Teutonic classicism, partly merely a matter of patriotic sentiment. Similarly with the twentieth-century revival, but that now the motive of cultural revolt is paramount. As never before the great heritage of the world's folk-songs has been collected and docketed. As never before an attempt has been made to create out of modal melody an idiom which would constitute an escape from the tyranny of the dominant seventh.

Bartók sought release from this tyranny in the folk-songs of Balkan Europe and North Africa, many of which have to a Western ear an exotic, barbaric character. Thus the sharpened sub-dominant of the Lydian mode forms with the tonic that interval of the tritone which, as we saw, medieval theorists called the 'diabolus in musica'. This interval figures prominently in the Lydian folk-songs of Slovakia. So it does in the important opening bars of Bartók's Fifth Quartet, in which after hammering out a B♮:

Ex. 156

the theme winds its way up to an accented E♮:

Ex. 157

Regarding Bartók's harmony, and that of Vaughan Williams, the other outstanding exponent of the trend, one can say broadly that neo-modal melody led to a novel individual form of chromaticism. We saw above that chromaticism, precisely because it produced a disrupting abnormal effect, was necessary to the major-minor system; we saw also that specific conditions of entry were imposed and that certain chromatic triads enjoyed the status of privileged foreigners (see Chapter XI). In the nature of the case a modal idiom sets up different norms of chromaticism. For instance, take the example I gave above of the Phrygian mode of C with its flattened super-tonic, D♭. In this mode a major triad on D♭ would be diatonic; in C minor, on the other hand, this triad would be a chromatic one (it would in fact be the chord referred to in my chapter on the chromatic triads as the Neapolitan Sixth, a 'fascinating foreigner', enjoying a special right of entry). On the other hand a chord such as the B♭ major triad, which contains a D♮ but not a D♭, is diatonic in C minor and chromatic in the Phrygian mode of C.

Thus the very fact of writing in a mode sets up a different criterion of what is and is not chromatic. In their large-scale works, however, Bartók and Vaughan Williams do very much more than merely confine themselves to a single mode: they range freely from mode to mode, sometimes roping in the major and minor, sometimes combining two or more modes 'polymodally'. Thus the norms of their chromaticism are constantly shifting ones. We are at large in a world of—from the point of view of the major-minor system (which, of course, no longer obtains, since the terms of thought are modal)— startling chromatic transitions.

On the vast difference, their common neo-modalism notwithstanding, between the idioms of these two composers I can only touch briefly here. Partly it is due to the specifically Balkan features of Bartók's style: the florid chromatic ornaments, the irregular rhythms, the dynamic ostinato figures, the repeated notes (as witness the above example from the Fifth Quartet). Also Bartók's harmonic idiom is nearer to the post-Wagnerian romantic tradition than Vaughan Williams's: it is more highly wrought, more tense, more dissonant. Vaughan Williams's neo-modalism is purer: his modal themes tend to preserve the essentially lyrical character of the folk-songs from which they derive and the harmonies they evoke, however chromatic from the major-minor point of view, tend to be straightforward and euphonious. Indeed one can say of Vaughan Williams that through neo-modalism he found a way of giving a fresh lease of life to the common chord. As witness the meltingly beautiful penultimate bars of the *Romanza* of the Fifth Symphony. For a moment the melody lingers in the Mixolydian mode of A:

Ex. 158

The modal flavour of the melody is brought out by the sounding above it of the minor triad of G, its characteristically Mixolydian flattened leading note. In the world of the conventional A major mode the minor triad of G was utterly foreign; here in this Mixolydian world Vaughan Williams is making it at home.

Schoenberg's twelve-note system

Of the two 'independent rivers' (as I termed them above) constructed in the twentieth century by Schoenberg and Hindemith, the twelve-note system has infiltrated the farther. Not only did its drastically revolutionary character cause an immense stir in the experimental twenties and thirties; it has had a widespread, permeating effect upon the whole trend of contemporary harmony away from the classical tradition. Furthermore, it is a river which is still flowing—more strongly perhaps than ever. Not only in Germany and Austria, but in this country, France, Italy, and elsewhere a number of composers still employ the system and firmly believe in its possibilities.

The early works of Schoenberg (1874–1951) were couched in the post-Wagnerian romantic idiom. Already in the first decade of the century he had carried its chromaticism and dissonance to a point of atonality, i.e. to a point at which it became an idiom not merely modifying the basic structural principle of tonality, as it had been hitherto felt and understood, but dispensing with it altogether. He discarded the triad, the dominant seventh and dominant discords, and with them the whole classical apparatus of resolution by means of the appoggiatura and passing chord. Not only that, he employed a type of melody no longer based, as hitherto all Western melody had been, upon a diatonic scale, major, minor, modal or otherwise, but an unrestricted type enjoying the freedom of the chromatic scale and using this freedom to throw into relief the 'non-acoustic' interval-progressions—above all the acutely dissonant tritone and major seventh. As witness these bars from the songs from Stefan George's *Buch der hängenden Gärten*, Op. 15:

Ex. 159

In his *Style and Idea* Schoenberg makes it clear that the purpose of the twelve-note system was to order this atonal music through a principle which would replace tonality. The music, he says, had been conceived 'as in a dream'; it forced upon him the task of exploring the logic which underlay it. 'After many unsuccessful attempts during a period of approximately twelve years, I laid the foundations for a new procedure in musical construction which seemed fitted to replace those structural differentiations provided formerly by tonal harmonies.'[1]

The principle of this 'new procedure' was to construct not only the melody, but the entire contrapuntal *and harmonic*

[1] *Style and Idea*, p. 107.

texture of a piece upon the framework of a given series of twelve notes. The series was conceived of as existing in four different forms: in its original form; in the inversion of its original form; in so-called mirror form (i.e. with the order of the notes reversed); and in the inversion of the mirror form. The melody would consist of nothing but a continuous repetition of the series in one or other of these forms. The composer, however, was free to transpose, to introduce whatever phrasing and rhythmic pattern he pleased, and to combine the various forms of the series in a freely dissonant counterpoint. Also he was free, if he so wished, to arrange the notes of his series vertically. Instead of presenting itself in the form of a melody, a series beginning with the notes, say, C, D♭, and B, could

Ex. 160

present itself in the form of a chord; thus:

This, of course, was the system's most drastically revolutionary feature.

Such a series, so handled, could, Schoenberg held, perform the centralizing function of a tonic—provided one vital condition was observed. The series must consist of all the twelve notes of the chromatic scale. If it contained more notes than the twelve, one would be continually being repeated and hence asserting itself as tonic at the expense of the series as a whole. And if it contained less than the twelve, the selected notes would convey an implication of specific chosen harmonic combinations acting as tonal centres in the old sense.

At the back of Schoenberg's belief that such a twelve-note series, permeating the entire substance of a work, could exert the integrating power of tonality seems to have lain a philosophic conception. In *Style and Idea*[1] he refers to music as a sphere in which '. . . as in Swedenborg's heaven . . . , there is no absolute down, no right or left, forward or backward. Every musical configuration . . . has to be comprehended primarily as a mutual relation of sounds . . . appearing at different times and places.' As the objects of the material world can be recognized or imagined in any position, so a musical creator's

[1] Page 113.

mind can operate subconsciously with a row of tones, regardless of their direction, regardless of the way in which a mirror might show the mutual relations, which remain a given quantity.

Within the limited space of this sub-section I can do no more than give this very bald outline of the twelve-note system. It is capable of a multitude of refinements and modifications; and from some of these it would appear that the intended break with the past need not after all be absolute. Thus Alban Berg (1885–1935) in his Violin Concerto used a series consisting mainly of triads and went out of his way to demonstrate the possibility of a synthesis between twelve-note and tonal harmony. The system is in fact a flexible one and there is a tendency among twelve-note composers today to relax some of Schoenberg's original conditions.[1] Whether its premises are valid; whether serial composing really is a subconscious mode of musical creation or merely a mechanical substitute for it, constructed in defiance of the nature of harmony and melody, has always been a matter of acute controversy. Into this I cannot enter here. Having described the system as impartially as I can (I am not a Schoenbergian) I leave it to the 'intelligent listener' to pass his own judgement on the validity of the theory and on the artistic value of the music to which it has given rise.[2]

Hindemith's system of harmony

Whereas the motive of Schoenberg's system, displacing the triad, was revolutionary, that of Hindemith's is evolutionary: he seeks not to displace the triad but to construct a new harmonic framework in which its tonal functioning could have a wider range. Conventional harmony, taking cognizance as it does only of triads and dominant discords on the one hand and inessential passing and appoggiatura chords on the other, is, Hindemith complains, too narrow: many other chords are there for the using but, as he puts it, 'there is no room in a well-ordered house for such rabble'.[3] What is needed, he

---

[1] Thus Dallapiccola in his opera *Il Prigoniero* uses more than one series; and in his song cycle *Quattro Liriche* a scale-like series with modal implications.

[2] The reader will find fuller accounts of the system in Grove and in Mosco Carner's *A Study of Twentieth-Century Harmony*; and still fuller ones, with examples of the various methods of Schoenberg, Berg, and Webern (1883–1945), in *Style and Idea* and Humphrey Searle's *Twentieth-Century Counterpoint*.

[3] *The Craft of Musical Composition*, p. 106.

concludes, is a complete re-thinking and re-systematization of the chordal vocabulary, throwing it open to the composer in search of new harmonic forms.

The basic feature of Hindemith's system is a novel conception of the working of tonality. In the classical system tonality manifests itself in the sense of key binding into a unit the diatonic notes and fundamental chords of the major and minor scales. Hindemith abolishes key and constructs in its place a theoretic graduated series of tonal relationships between a central tonic and *every* other note of the chromatic scale. He arrives at this series by means of an elaborate analysis of overtone-relationships; its validity is debatable, but it has the merit of making it possible to regard any chord, no matter how *outré* from the conventional point of view, as in principle related to a central tonic and accordingly available.

Not that the system allows a composer the free run of any and every chord. Hindemith views with horror the chromatic anarchy into which post-Wagnerian romantic harmony lapsed and the twelve-note method of ordering it in defiance of the realities of acoustics. To him these realities are inescapable. Of the major triad he writes that it is '. . . to the trained and the naïve listener alike one of the most impressive phenomena of nature, simple and elemental as rain, snow and wind. . . The musician cannot escape it any more than the painter his primary colours, or the architect his three dimensions. . . In the world of tones, the triad corresponds to the force of gravity. It serves as our constant guiding point, our unit of measure, and our goal, even in those sections of compositions which avoid it.'[1]

In Hindemith's system of 'diatonicized chromaticism' (as it has been called) the major triad does indeed serve as a 'constant guiding point' and 'unit of measure'. Thus in his book, *The Craft of Musical Composition*, he gives a complete list of all types of chords, measured and compared according to the acoustic quality of the intervals they contain. Thus he lays down that the line formed by the roots of a chordal progression must contain a modicum of fifths and fourths—acoustically the two 'best' intervals—if it is to define a tonal centre. Thus he lays down—and here he departs drastically from con-

[1] *The Craft of Musical Composition*, p. 22.

ventional theory—that the root of a chord is the root of its acoustically 'best' interval. The root, for example, of this chromatic agglomeration (I quote from Hindemith's book)[1]

Ex. 161

is A, since this note is the root of the fifth,

A–E, its 'best' interval. Since for Hindemith the root of a chord, thus derived, is the note which defines its place within a tonal design, the chord in question, its chromaticism notwithstanding, could be 'diatonicized' by placing it in a passage of which the centre of the tonal design is A.

In singling out this particular feature of Hindemith's system, basically important though it is, I am, of course, doing him an injustice. To be understood the system must be grasped in its complicated entirety, with those features which resemble and those which depart from conventional harmony clearly distinguished. Having done so one may perhaps still consider that a fallacy lurks behind it all; that it is one thing to exploit the major triad, as conventional harmony does, *in conjunction with* melody and rhythm, and quite another to build it up as the focal point of a harmonic system derived from a study of acoustics. Yet though the counterblast to Schoenberg's iconoclasm may not ring true, one cannot but pay tribute to the motive prompting it; cannot but feel that there is something challenging and heartening in Hindemith's belief that the harmony of the great past is not a dead letter, but a heritage still capable of further expansion and development.[2]

[1] *The Craft of Musical Composition*, p. 97.
[2] An adequate idea of Hindemith's system can only be acquired from Hindemith's own *The Craft of Musical Composition*, though the above-mentioned works by Mosco Carner and Humphrey Searle contain helpful accounts.

CHAPTER XVIII

Conclusion

HAVING completed our survey of the proliferating trends of the twentieth century, let us finally make our way back to the main stream of classical harmony and broadly review the pattern of its course which we have been tracing through this book.

We traced it through several stages. We started by showing the fundamental principle of tonality in embryo. We analysed the tune of the National Anthem and saw that it was informed by a logic of 'departure in order to return' built up by phrases moving to cadence notes other than the tonic. Then we classified the intervals and showed how their different qualities —revealed on the one hand in the relation between the cadence's final note and the tonic, and on the other in that between the penultimate and final notes of the cadence— governed the working of this logic.

Having occupied this vantage ground we could then advance into the territory of harmony proper. We analysed the concords of the major scale and showed that as the relation of final cadence note to tonic was differentiated by the quality of the interval they formed, so the relation of final cadence chord to chord of tonic was differentiated by the degree of 'likeness' of the two concords. Then we passed on to consider the harmonic cadences and to observe above all the pivotal thrust of the chord of the dominant to that of the tonic. The harmonic cadences, we saw, imparted to the major and minor scales the quality of integration expressed in the word 'key', a quality giving rise to the resource of key change immensely widening the scope of the logic of tonality.

We then turned to consider discords. We started by adopting the point of view of the sixteenth-century polyphonists and introducing dissonances to impart force and variety to separate strands of counterpoint. We drew a distinction between the interpolated inessential note and passing chord on the one hand, and on the other the more expressive highly charged suspension and appoggiatura, which fell on a strong beat and made good the intrusion by resolving melodically. We singled out the dominant seventh available on the dominant of a major and minor key and showed how it was a discord capable of powerfully reinforcing the chord of the dominant's thrust to that of the tonic, which was the pivotal feature of the key system.

The role of the dominant seventh once understood, our discussion was free to advance on to the wider stage of key change. First we dealt with the bare mechanism of a change: the 'establishing' of a new key by its dominant seventh, with or without a modulating chord. Then we distinguished various types of change: the passing and the cadential types, and the type definitively leading to a passage in a new key. We distinguished also between changes to related and to remote keys and observed that passing and cadential changes to a related key do not really convey a shift of tonality, but that their effect is rather to expand the range of a single key.

Before going on to deal with remote key changes it was necessary to give some consideration to the chromatic triads and to chromaticism generally. We saw that chromatic notes provided an essential element of expressive variety and that they were subject to the same terms of admission as dissonant ones, i.e. they must function melodically. We then identified certain chromatic triads so commonly used that they could be regarded as part of the stock vocabulary of a key.

Resuming the topic of key change, we remarked that it was not until the reaction which set in in the eighteenth century against the contrapuntal idiom of Bach and Handel, based mainly on a scheme of changes only to related keys, that the remote key change came into its own, bringing about the full expansion of the key system in the sonata-form of the Vienna Classics. We saw how in sonata-form the mainspring of this expansion was the shift of tonality to a point of extreme departure created by the remote key changes of the development section. Then we dwelt upon the part which modulation played. A key, we saw, could be regarded as the focal centre of a tonal system formed by its five satellite related keys. On the wide stage of sonata-form modulation was called upon to perform the task of destroying a related key's character as satellite and setting it up as the centre of its own tonal system. We saw—at first schematically, and then by analysing the first movement of Mozart's 'Jupiter' Symphony—what a rich and vital resource this form of modulation was; how a new tonal system could be built up rapidly or gradually, and with varying degrees of thoroughness; how, in the case of a remote key, it could be reached with breath-taking suddenness; how an extended modulation by 'doubling on its tracks' could create a powerful effect of tonal ambiguity.

The detailed analysis I gave of the tonal and thematic structure of the first movement of the 'Jupiter' was the climax of the first part of this unconventional textbook. With it I attained my object of showing how the key system, exploited on the widest possible scale, was the dimension in which the Vienna Classics conceived their masterpieces. There now remained the further task of showing how, modified and transformed by chromaticism, the system produced the romantic idiom of the nineteenth century.

We subjected the dominant seventh to further investigation. It could, we saw, act as the resolving chord of a number of appoggiatura chords, among which we singled out the dominant major and minor ninths and the diminished seventh. The major ninth, we saw, had a yearning bitter-sweet expressiveness which in the nineteenth century was given its head; furthermore, it was used to resolve still more highly charged appoggiatura chords. In the classical idiom, in which key change was an essential term of thought, the fundamental harmony of the triad and dominant seventh had been implied by a movement's themes and had imbued its whole harmonic texture; in the romantic idiom fundamental harmony was being treated as the basis of intensely expressive sensuously beautiful appoggiatura harmonies clogging a movement's rhythm and blurring its tonal design. We turned then to the enharmonic diminished seventh and saw that in the hands of the romantics it was made to serve the same effects; that an enharmonic modulation abolished tonal space, the dimension of classical sonata-form; that it transformed the chequer board of the Viennese masters into a kaleidoscope of shifting tonality.

Our next step was to observe how these tendencies were

carried still further when the dominant seventh, instead of proceeding to the tonic chord to which it thrusts, was quitted chromatically. We saw how in the form of an augmented sixth it could become the vehicle of an enharmonic modulation. Finally, we analysed a passage from *Tristan* consisting of a whole series of dominant discords of different type resolving appoggiatura-wise upon a succession of dominant sevenths drawn from different keys. In this passage we found the apotheosis of romantic harmony: the dominant seventh which for the Viennese masters was the dynamic agent of a long-term harmonic-thematic argument was being employed together with its derivative appoggiatura chords to charge a few bars with the utmost romantic eloquence.

At the risk of appearing to make a digression, I then felt it incumbent upon me to indicate some of the ways in which the symphonic masters of the nineteenth century brought about a synthesis between classical sonata-form and the inimical tendencies of romanticism. Discussing works of Schubert, Tchaikovsky, and Brahms I showed how the power of a movement could lie less in its tonal design than in the wealth of its melodic contrast and in the force of its melodic expressiveness, raised to a new potency by the appoggiaturing dominant discords of the harmony and by the sensuous impact of orchestral tone-colour.

Finally I devoted a chapter to some of the principal trends of harmony in the twentieth century. The majority of those I dealt with were, I tried to show, in the nature of streams flowing out of the main river of classical harmony, developing its latent possibilities. Schoenberg's and Hindemith's systems were, on the other hand, independent constructions. The subject was so wide that the chapter itself inevitably had the character of a summary. I need not, therefore, touch upon it any further here.

And so at length we reach the end of this review of the course of harmony, and with it the end of this book. As I said in my Introduction I have aimed at 'taking harmony . . . out of the textbook and opening a window on the whole by showing its interconnection with melody, form, style, and the history and psychology of music'. So doing I have, I hope, conveyed some understanding of how harmony works, of how it seems to say one thing in the idiom of a Bach, another in that of a Beethoven, yet another in that of a Wagner, and still other and very different things in the various idioms of the twentieth century. I shall be content if the reader of these pages feels better able to understand the nature of his own reactions to all these manifold idioms; better able to frame and formulate his judgements and opinions; better able to turn to account the treasure which is his for the taking, if he can but take it—the accumulated heritage of musical art, in all its grandeur and complexity.

RECOMMENDED BOOKS

Eric Blom	*Everyman's Dictionary of Music*
Eric Blom	*The Limitations of Music*
Percy C. Buck	*The Scope of Music*
Mosco Carner	*A Study of Twentieth Century Harmony*
Deryck Cooke	*The Language of Music*
Alfred Einstein	*Greatness in Music*
Wilhelm Furtwaengler	*Concerning Music*
Alec Harman and Wilfrid Mellers	*Man and his Music*
Imogen Holst	*Tune*
Wilfrid Mellers	*Caliban Reborn*
Arnold Schoenberg	*Style and Idea*
Percy A. Scholes	*The Concise Oxford Dictionary of Music*
Percy A. Scholes	*The Oxford Companion to Music*
D. F. Tovey	*The Integrity of Music*
D. F. Tovey	*A Musician Talks*
D. F. Tovey	*Essays in Musical Analysis*
Alan Walker	*An Anatomy of Musical Criticism*
Bruno Walter	*Of Music and Music-making*
R. Vaughan Williams	*The Making of Music*
Victor Zuckerkandl	*The Sense of Music*

INDEX

PRINTED LITHOGRAPHICALLY BY HEADLEY BROTHERS LTD THE INVICTA PRESS ASHFORD KENT